GUIDED FLIGHT DISCOVERY
PRIVATE PILOT MANEUVERS

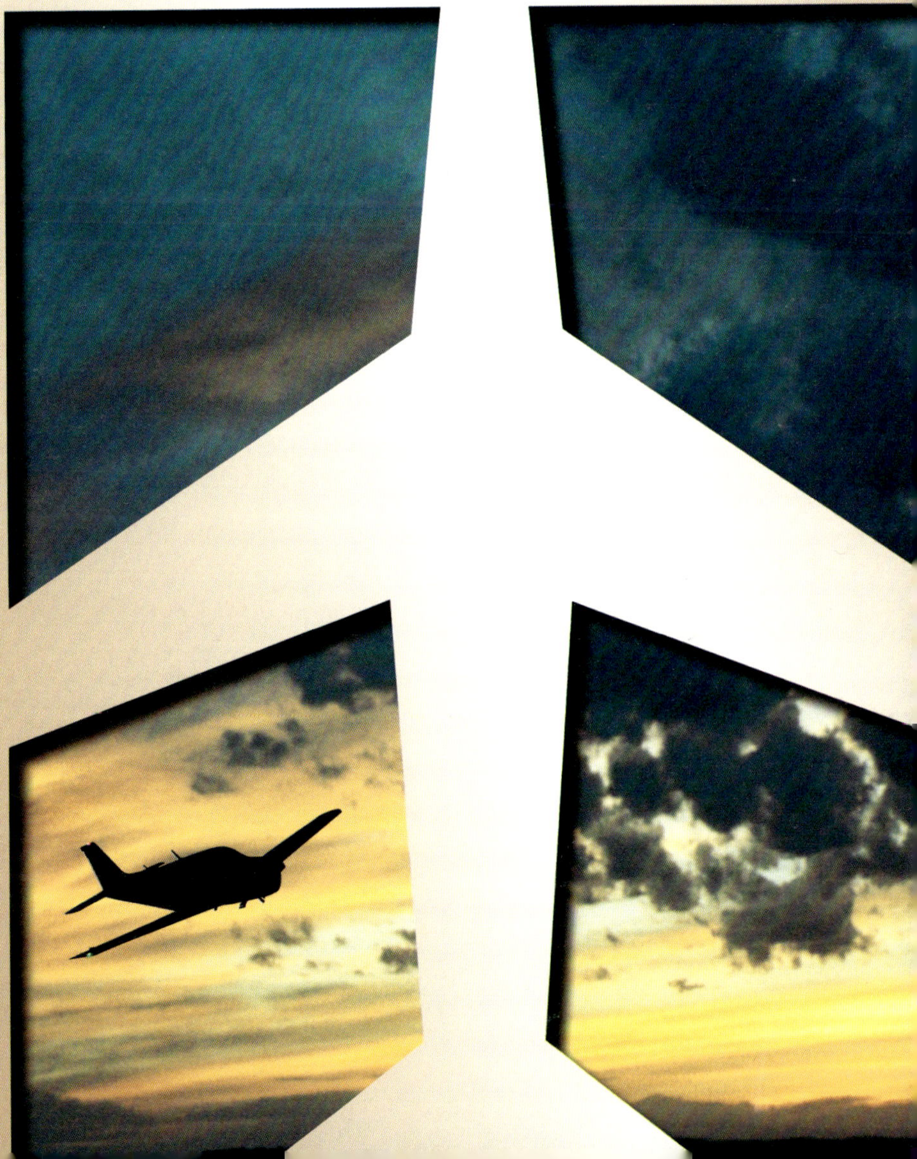

Jeppesen® is a registered trademark of Jeppesen Sanderson, Inc. All other trademarks, registered trademarks, product names, and company names or logos mentioned herein are the property of their respective owners.

All rights reserved. No part of this publication may be reproduced, stored in a retrieval system, or transmitted in any form or by any means, electronic, mechanical, photocopying, recording, or otherwise, without the prior permission of the publisher.

The charts, tables, and graphs used in this publication are for illustration purposes only and cannot be used for navigation or to determine actual aircraft performance.

ISBN: 978-0-88487-610-6

Jeppesen
55 Inverness Drive East
Englewood, CO 80112-5498
Web site: www.jeppesen.com
Email: Captain@jeppesen.com
Copyright © Jeppesen
All Rights Reserved.
Published 1997-2007, 2011, 2012, 2013
Printed in the United States of America

PREFACE

All of the individual components of Jeppesen's Guided Flight Discovery Pilot Training System concentrate on an application-oriented approach to pilot training. Nothing exemplifies this philosophy more than *Private Pilot Maneuvers*. When used in conjunction with the other components of the Private Pilot Program, this manual provides an effective, practical approach to your training. As you examine this manual, you will discover that the maneuvers are numbered for ease of reference and are grouped into categories based on similar operational characteristics. While the categories are organized to present the maneuvers in the chronological order in which they are typically introduced, this does not limit the flexibility and usability of the manual; you can study and review the maneuvers in any order you desire.

Each maneuver is presented using colorful graphics, step-by-step procedure descriptions, helpful hints, and the associated FAA practical test standards. In addition, *Private Pilot Maneuvers* is designed to lay flat for ease of study and instruction, whether you are on the ground or in flight. These, and other unique features of the manual, are explained in further detail in the section titled "How the Manual Works" starting on page vi.

To help you integrate the content of this manual with the associated Private Pilot Maneuvers Videos and CD-ROMs, a cross-reference is included at the beginning of each maneuver category. The video and CD-ROM programs are available for your use at participating schools and are designed to enhance and complement your study. You also can purchase the Private Pilot Maneuvers CD-ROMs for self-paced home study. These revolutionary CD-ROMs combine video, animation, and interactivity to create a dynamic learning experience. When used together, the components of the Guided Flight Discovery Private Pilot Program provide the finest pilot training available.

Table Of Contents

GROUND OPERATIONS
MANEUVER 1
- Preflight Inspection 1-2

MANEUVER 2
- Engine Starting 1-6

MANEUVER 3
- Taxiing 1-8

MANEUVER 4
- Before Takeoff Check 1-12

MANEUVER 5
- Postflight Procedures 1-16

EXERCISES
- Ground Operations 1-21

BASIC MANEUVERS
MANEUVER 6
- Straight-and-level Flight 2-2

MANEUVER 7
- Climbs 2-4

MANEUVER 8
- Descents 2-6

MANEUVER 9
- Turns 2-8

EXERCISES
- Basic Maneuvers 2-13

AIRPORT OPERATIONS
MANEUVER 10
- Normal Takeoff and Climb 3-2

MANEUVER 11
- Crosswind Takeoff and Climb 3-4

MANEUVER 12
- Traffic Patterns 3-6

MANEUVER 13
- Normal Approach and Landing 3-12

MANEUVER 14
- Crosswind Approach and Landing 3-20

EXERCISES
- Airport Operations 3-23

EMERGENCY LANDING PROCEDURES
MANEUVER 15
- Systems an Equipment Malfunctions 4-2

MANEUVER 16
- Emergency Desent 4-4

MANEUVER 17
- Emergency Approach and Landing 4-6

EXERCISES
- Emergency Landing Procedures 4-11

FLIGHT MANEUVERS

MANEUVER 18
Slow Flight 5-2

MANEUVER 19
Power-Off Stalls 5-4

MANEUVER 20
Power-On Stalls 5-8

MANEUVER 21
Demonstrated Stalls 5-11

MANEUVER 22
Steep Turns 5-14

EXERCISES
Flight Maneuvers 5-17

GROUND REFERENCE MANEUVERS

MANEUVER 23
Rectangular Course 6-2

MANEUVER 24
S-Turns 6-4

MANEUVER 25
Turns Around a Point 6-6

EXERCISES
Ground Reference Maneuvers 6-9

PERFORMANCE TAKEOFFS AND LANDINGS

MANEUVER 26
Short-Field Takeoff and Climb 7-2

MANEUVER 27
Short-Field Approach and Landing 7-4

MANEUVER 28
Soft-Field Takeoff and Climb 7-6

MANEUVER 29
Soft-Field Approach and Landing 7-8

EXERCISES
Performance Takeoffs and Landings 7-11

SPECIAL FLIGHT OPERATIONS

MANEUVER 30
Attitude Instrument Flying 8-2

MANEUVER 31
Night Operations 8-10

EXERCISES
Special Flight Operations 8-15

ANSWERS A-1

How the Manual Works

Private Pilot Maneuvers uses colorful graphics and step-by-step procedure descriptions to help you visualize and understand each maneuver you will perform in the airplane. Additional guidance is provided through insets which contain helpful hints, common errors, and FAA practical test standards. To get the most out of this manual, as well as the entire Guided Flight Discovery Pilot Training System, you may find it beneficial to review the major design elements in this text.

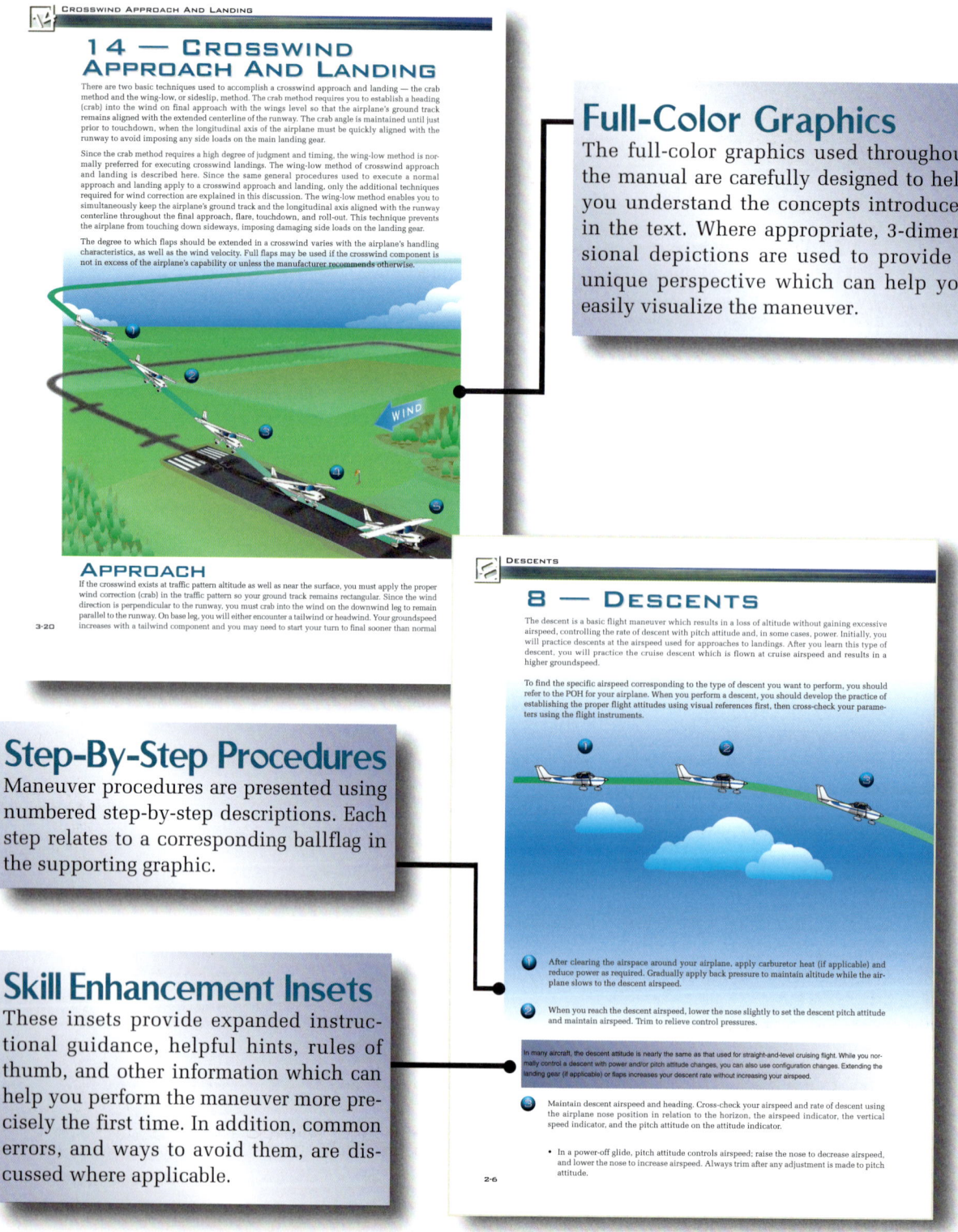

Full-Color Graphics
The full-color graphics used throughout the manual are carefully designed to help you understand the concepts introduced in the text. Where appropriate, 3-dimensional depictions are used to provide a unique perspective which can help you easily visualize the maneuver.

Step-By-Step Procedures
Maneuver procedures are presented using numbered step-by-step descriptions. Each step relates to a corresponding ballflag in the supporting graphic.

Skill Enhancement Insets
These insets provide expanded instructional guidance, helpful hints, rules of thumb, and other information which can help you perform the maneuver more precisely the first time. In addition, common errors, and ways to avoid them, are discussed where applicable.

TAXIING

QUARTERING TAILWINDS

A quartering tailwind is the most critical wind condition for taxiing a tricycle gear, high-wing airplane. Since quartering tailwinds have a tendency to flow beneath the elevator (or stabilator) and lift the tail, the airplane may tip over on the nosewheel and one main wheel.

① Fully turn the yoke in the direction away from the wind. In a right quartering tailwind turn the yoke fully to the left, or left aileron up. Reverse the position of the aileron control when taxiing with a left quartering tailwind.

② Hold the yoke full forward to maintain the elevator (or stabilator) in a down position which will counteract the airplane's tipping tendency.

Be particularly cautious when you are slowing down and beginning a turn in a quartering tailwind. The increasing tailwind component, combined with the normal tendency of the airplane to tip during the turn, makes the airplane especially vulnerable to being overturned. Slow taxi speeds and slow turns minimize this danger.

 TAXIING

To meet the PTS requirements, you must:

- Exhibit knowledge of the elements related to safe taxi procedures.
- Position the flight controls properly for the existing wind conditions.
- Perform a brake check immediately after the airplane begins to move.
- Control direction and speed without excessive use of brakes.
- Comply with airport markings, signals, and ATC clearances.
- Avoid other aircraft and hazards.
- Complete the appropriate checklist.

PTS Insets
The FAA practical test standards associated with each maneuver are presented in an inset at the end of the maneuver description.

EXERCISES — GROUND OPERATIONS

1 — PREFLIGHT INSPECTION

1. What should you use to ensure that all steps are completed when performing a preflight inspection? _____
2. What documents are required on board the airplane? _____
3. How can you tell when water is present in a fuel sample? _____
4. True/False. Nicks on the propeller can cause excessive stress and should be checked by a certificated mechanic. _____
5. What documents are not required to be on board the airplane? _____
   A. Airworthiness certificate, aircraft logbooks
   B. Airworthiness directives (ADs), maintenance records
   C. Airworthiness directives (ADs), approved flight manual

2 — ENGINE STARTING

1. True/False. Before you start the engine, a thorough look around the propeller eliminates the need for opening a window or door and shouting "CLEAR!" _____
2. The primer pumps fuel into what part of the engine? _____
3. Where would you find procedural information on starting the airplane with an external power source? _____
4. After you start the engine in cold weather, the oil pressure should register properly within how many seconds? _____
5. After starting the engine, what action should you take in the event the oil pressure does not register within the green arc in the recommended time? _____

3 — TAXIING

The following questions pertain to a tricycle gear airplane.

1. True/False. Taxi speed is primarily controlled by using the brakes. _____
2. Does the effectiveness of the aileron, rudder, and elevator (or stabilator) controls increase or decrease as the airplane's speed decreases? _____

Exercises
Exercises follow each of the eight tabbed categories to help you evaluate your understanding of each maneuver presented. Answers are provided at the end of the manual.

GROUND OPERATIONS

GROUND OPERATIONS

GROUND OPERATIONS

MANEUVER 1 1-2
   PREFLIGHT INSPECTION

MANEUVER 2 1-6
   ENGINE STARTING

MANEUVER 3 1-8
   TAXIING

MANEUVER 4 1-12
   BEFORE TAKEOFF CHECK

MANEUVER 5 1-16
   POSTFLIGHT PROCEDURES

EXERCISES 1-21

Video Volume I — Ground Operations, Basic Maneuvers, Airport Operations, and Emergency Landing Procedures

Computer Training — Ground Operations

Since there can be vast differences in ground operations from one airplane to another, the procedures in this section are intentionally general in nature. Therefore, it is imperative that you use an appropriate printed checklist which provides a logical step-by-step sequence for each task you will perform.

PREFLIGHT INSPECTION

1 — PREFLIGHT INSPECTION

As a pilot, you are the final authority regarding the airworthiness and safe operation of your aircraft. Your flight instructor will point out the various components to be inspected and explain how to determine the airworthiness of the airplane. In addition, the pilot's operating handbook (POH) normally contains a checklist and other information regarding the preflight inspection. If a discrepancy is discovered during your preflight inspection, it should be evaluated and, if required, corrected prior to the flight. You may need to enlist the assistance of an aviation maintenance technician to answer questions or resolve problems that you find while inspecting the airplane.

Prior to performing a visual inspection of the airplane, you should check the aircraft logbooks and records to ensure that the appropriate airworthiness directives have been complied with, maintenance requirements have been met, and aircraft inspections have been performed. Airworthiness directives (ADs) require correction of unsafe conditions found in engines, propellers, and other equipment. ADs also prescribe the conditions under which the affected equipment may continue to be operated. Records of AD compliance and the aircraft logbooks are not required to be on board the aircraft.

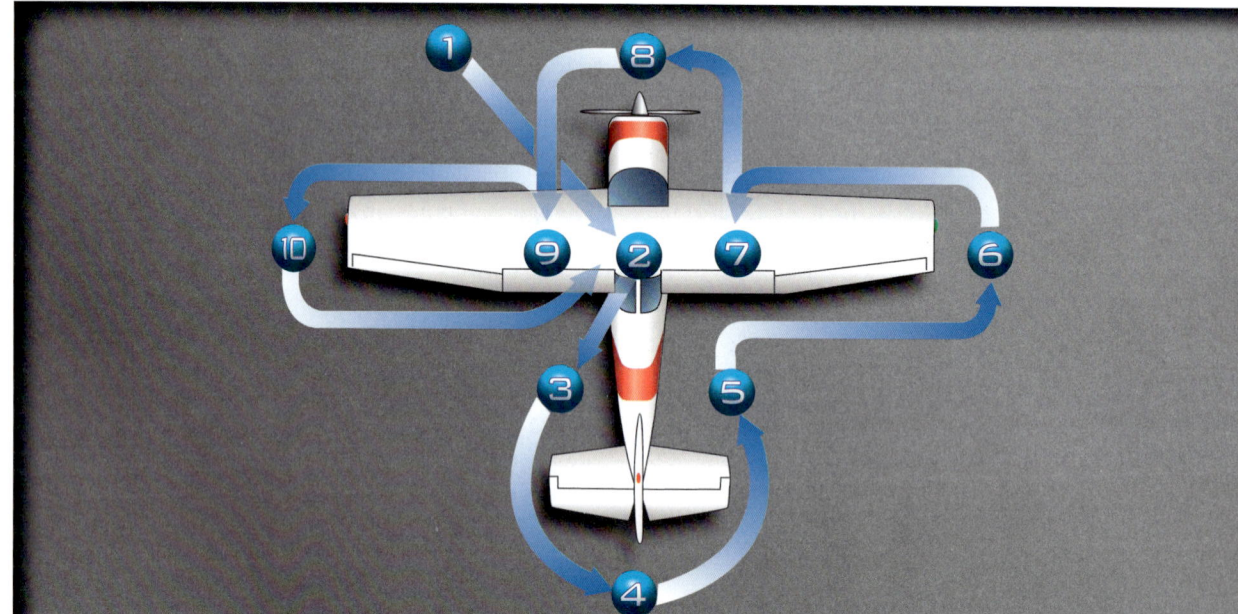

 Your preflight inspection should begin as you walk toward the airplane. This provides you with an overall look at the airplane that may indicate items you will want to inspect more closely during your walkaround. During the winter months, you should remove all frost, snow, and ice accumulations from the airplane surfaces.

 ### IN CABIN

- In the cabin, verify that all the required paperwork is on board the airplane. Use the acronym **ARROW** to help you remember the required documents.

    Airworthiness certificate (required by FAA)

    Registration certificate (required by FAA)

    Radio station class license (required by the Federal Communications Commission when transmitting to ground stations outside the United States)

    Operating instructions, pilot's operating handbook, or approved aircraft flight manual (required by FAA)

    Weight and Balance data, as well as equipment list (required by FAA)

Preflight Inspection

Although typically not issued for light aircraft, you may encounter an airplane which has an approved minimum equipment list (MEL). The MEL is an inventory of instruments and equipment that may legally be inoperative. If your airplane has an approved MEL, you need to know what instruments and equipment are required, how to operate the airplane with inoperative components, and the procedures for obtaining a special flight permit.

- Next, remove the control lock and check the controls for freedom of movement.
- Clear the propeller area, and then turn the master switch ON.
- Verify proper operation of fuel gauges and note the fuel quantity in each tank.
- Lower the flaps and turn the master switch OFF.
- Inspect the instrument panel for any irregularities, such as cracked glass or any equipment which may have been removed for maintenance.
- Ensure the windscreen and windows are clean and in good condition.
- Before continuing to the exterior inspection, verify that the magneto switch, master switch, mixture control, and throttle are in the OFF position.

 ## Fuselage (left side)

- Moving toward the tail, visually inspect the left side of the fuselage for skin wrinkles, dents, and loose rivets.

External damage, such as wrinkled skin, may indicate internal structural damage.

- Check the lower surface of the fuselage for evidence of engine oil leakage, dents, and general condition.
- If a static port is located on the fuselage, check for obstructions.

During cleaning or waxing of the airplane, the static port can become plugged. It is important that the static source be open for proper operation of the airspeed indicator, altimeter, and vertical speed indicator.

 ## Empennage

- Remove the external rudder lock (if installed).
- Inspect the tail surfaces for general condition, looking closely for skin wrinkles, dents, and loose rivets.
- Examine the rudder for damage, loose hinge bolts, and freedom of movement.
- Closely inspect the control cables and stops for damage.
- Visually inspect the flashing beacon, tail light, and VOR navigation antenna on the vertical stabilizer for damage.
- Examine the elevator (or stabilator) trim tab, checking for security and general condition.
- For tailwheel airplanes, check the steering arms, cables, and springs for wear. Additionally, inspect the tire for wear, cuts, abrasions, and proper inflation.
- Lastly, remove the tail tiedown chain or rope.

 ## Fuselage (right side)

- Inspect the right side fuselage, as before, looking for skin wrinkles, dents, and loose rivets.

Right Wing

- Thoroughly inspect the wing flap for general condition and the flap hinges for security.

Preflight Inspection

- If the flap track is visible, check to ensure it is in good condition and does not show unusual wear.
- Inspect the aileron surfaces for dents and skin wrinkles and the hinges for security, damage, and freedom of movement.
- Check the aileron pushrod or cables for security, damage, and tension.
- Check the right wingtip for damage and secure attachment, and inspect the right navigation light.
- Examine the leading edge of the wing for dents or other damage.
- Inspect the upper surface of the wing for wrinkles or dents which may indicate internal structural damage.
- Next, remove the fuel cap and visually check the fuel quantity. In addition to ensuring that the fuel quantity is sufficient for the proposed flight, you should verify that the fuel level agrees with the fuel quantity gauge indication observed earlier.
- Before replacing the fuel cap, inspect the rubber gasket for cracks or deterioration.
- Inspect the fuel vent in the filler cap for obstructions, and then replace the filler cap and tighten it securely.
- Use your fuel tester to take a fuel sample from the fuel tank drain and check the color to verify that the fuel is the proper grade. If water or other contaminants are found in the sample, continue draining fuel until there is no evidence of contamination.

> Water can form in the fuel tanks from condensation of moisture in the air, or it may be present in the fuel added to the tanks. Since water is heavier than aviation fuel, it will settle to the bottom of the fuel tester.

- Remove the wing tiedown rope or chain.

Landing Gear (right side)

- Inspect the skin around the attachment points of the main landing gear for dents and wrinkles.
- Examine the tire for proper inflation, cuts, and condition of the tread.
- Check the wheel fairing (if installed) for cracks, dents, and security.
- Inspect the brake pads for wear and the hydraulic brake lines for security and leaks.
- If your airplane is equipped with oleo struts, ensure proper strut inflation.

Nose

- Open the cowl access door to inspect the engine components for loose wires and clamps, worn hoses, and oil or fuel leaks.
- Determine the oil quantity by removing and reading the dipstick. Add oil if the level is below the minimum recommended by the manufacturer. Then, replace the dipstick and tighten it securely.
- Drain the fuel strainer (if located within the engine compartment) for several seconds to eliminate any water or contaminants.
- If there is a fuel drain directly below the fuel selector on the underside of the airplane, take a fuel sample and check for contamination.

> The fuel strainer is often the lowest point in the fuel system so any water present should accumulate in the strainer.

- Check the engine cowl for security.

Preflight Inspection

- Inspect the propeller and spinner for security and check the propeller for nicks and cracks.

Propeller nicks can cause excessive stress in the metal and should be repaired by an aviation technician prior to flight.

- If your airplane has a constant-speed propeller, check for oil leaks.

Oil leaks around the seals of constant-speed propellers can generally be detected by oil streaks on the back side of the propeller blades or oil spots on the cowling or windscreen.

- Examine the nosewheel tire for proper inflation, cuts, abrasions, and condition of the tread.
- Check the wheel fairing (if installed) for cracks, dents, and security.
- Carefully inspect the nosewheel strut for proper inflation, leaks, and security.
- Inspect the steering linkages for security and the shimmy damper for leaks or damage.
- Check the cowl flaps (if installed) for security.
- Check the exterior surface of the windshield for cleanliness and general condition.

To clean the windshield, use a clean soft cloth and a cleaning compound specifically designed for airplane windshields. A dry rag should not be used since it can scratch the windshield surface.

- If a static port is located on the cowling, check for obstructions.

 ## Landing Gear (Left Side)

- Examine the left main landing gear as you did the right main gear.

 ## Left Wing

- Inspect the left wing as you did the right wing.
- Examine the pitot tube for damage and check the opening for obstructions.

A plugged pitot tube opening will cause the airspeed indicator to malfunction.

- If the static port is located on the pitot tube, ensure it is clean and free of obstructions.
- Check the stall warning vane (if installed) for freedom of movement.

If you turn on the master switch just prior to the stall warning vane inspection, you can check the signal when the vane is deflected upward. Remember to turn the master switch off immediately after making this inspection.

- If the airplane is equipped with a pneumatic stall warning device, check the opening for obstructions.

 PREFLIGHT INSPECTION

To meet the PTS requirements, you must:

- Exhibit knowledge of the elements related to preflight inspection. This shall include which items must be inspected, the reasons for checking each item, and how to detect possible defects.
- Inspect the airplane with reference to an appropriate checklist.
- Verifiy that the airplane is in condition for safe flight.

2 — Engine Starting

Although engine starting procedures can vary from one make and model of airplane to another, there are some safety precautions which are common to most general aviation aircraft. You should avoid starting the engine with the tail of the airplane pointed toward people standing nearby, property on the ramp, open hangers, or other aircraft that could be damaged by the wind blast from the propeller. Inspect the ground under the propeller before you start the engine, especially if you are operating on an unimproved surface. Rocks, pebbles, or any other loose debris can be picked up by the propeller and cause damage to the blades or be hurled backward. Since there are a number of different procedures used to start airplane engines, it is very important to follow the appropriate printed checklist provided by the aircraft manufacturer. The POH normally contains a checklist and expanded procedures for engine starting.

① Place the carburetor heat control in the COLD position (if applicable).

② **Fuel-injected**—Set the mixture control to RICH.

ENGINE STARTING

3. **Non-fuel-injected**—use the engine primer to pump fuel into the intake system. The number of primer strokes required depends on the length of time the engine has been shut down and the temperature of the outside air. In cold weather, a greater number of primer strokes may be necessary than when operating in warmer temperatures. Refer to your airplane's POH for the manufacturer's recommendation. **Fuel-injected**—Prime the engine by turning on the fuel pump and opening the throttle 1/4 to 1/2 inch so that you observe an indication on the fuel-flow meter for several seconds, then pull the mixture control back to IDLE CUTOFF.

4. Open the throttle approximately 1/8 to 1/2 inch, depending on the manufacturer's recommendation.

5. Prior to starting the engine, ensure the area around the airplane is clear. Open a window or the door, call out, *"CLEAR,"* and listen for a response.

6. With the area clear, turn the master switch ON.

7. Turn the anti-collision lights on to provide a visual warning to people approaching the airplane that the engine is about to start.

8. Turn or press the ignition switch to engage the starter.
   Fuel-injected—Advance the mixture control to RICH as the engine fires.
   To avoid damage to the starter, return the switch to the BOTH position as soon as the engine starts.

During winter months it may be necessary to use an external power source to provide sufficient energy to start the engine. If your airplane is equipped with a ground service plug receptacle, carefully follow the procedures outlined in the POH.

9. Adjust the throttle to the recommended idle power setting.

10. Check the oil pressure gauge to ensure the oil pressure registers within the green arc. If the oil pressure does not register in the normal range within 30 seconds in warm weather or within 60 seconds in cold weather, immediately shut down the engine to prevent possible damage.

ENGINE STARTING

To meet the PTS requirements, you must:

- Exhibit knowledge of the elements related to recommended engine starting procedures. This shall include the use of an external power source, hand propping safety, and starting under various atmospheric conditions.

- Position the airplane properly considering structures, surface conditions, other aircraft, and the safety of nearby persons and property.

- Utilize the appropriate checklist for starting procedure.

3 — Taxiing

To become proficient at taxiing, you must learn directional control techniques and the proper throttle usage to control speed. To maneuver on the ground, most light training aircraft have a steerable nosewheel which is linked to the rudder pedals. The main landing gear usually have brakes which are differentially controlled by toe pressure on the rudder pedals. The ailerons are normally used to maintain control while taxiing in windy conditions. You should refer to the pilot's operating handbook and the appropriate checklist for specific taxi procedures for your airplane.

Basic Taxi Techniques

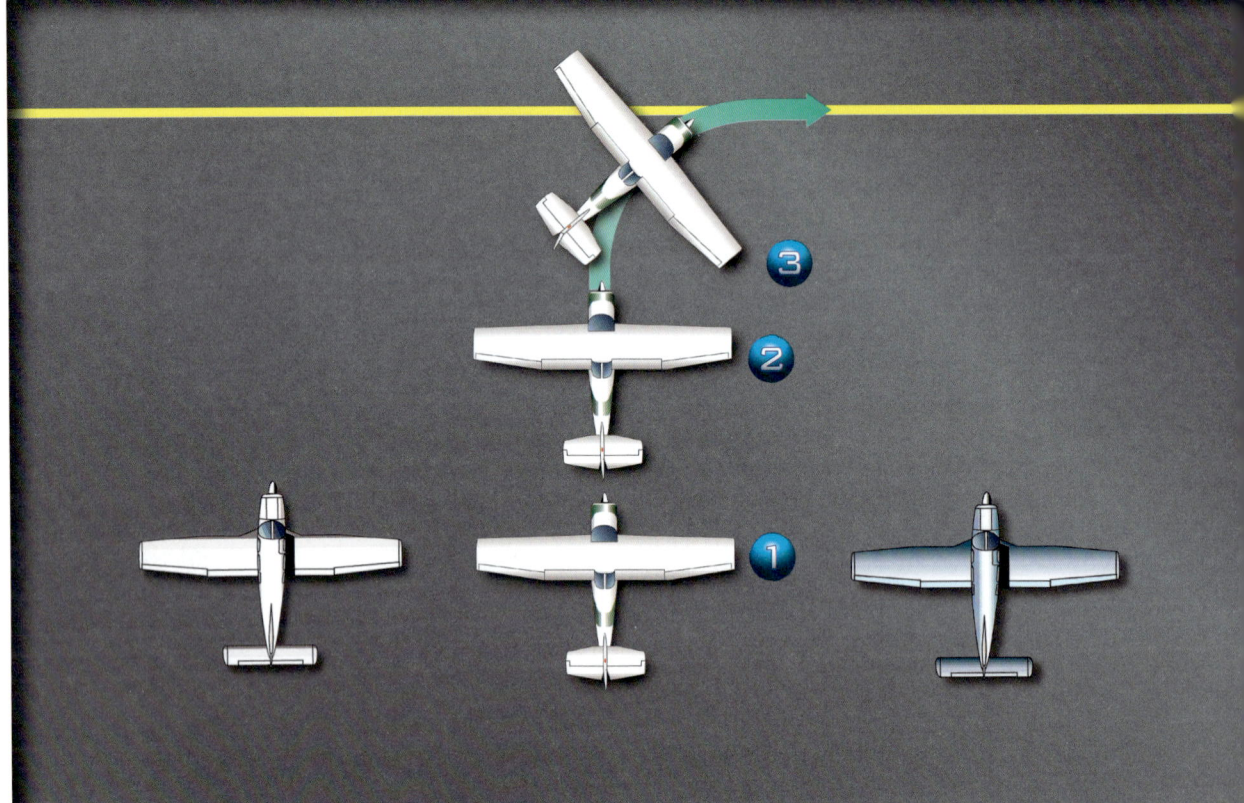

 Clear the area around the airplane. Add power slowly until the airplane begins rolling and then reduce power. More power is required to start the airplane rolling than is required to keep it rolling.

> A higher power setting is necessary to start and sustain an airplane in motion on a soft surface, such as grass, than on a hard surface.

 Test the brakes for proper operation and then readjust the power setting to obtain a normal taxi speed. Taxi speed is primarily controlled by the throttle and secondarily by the brakes. Use the brakes only when a reduction of engine r.p.m. is not sufficient to slow the airplane.

> Continually riding the brakes to control speed while taxiing may cause excessive wear or overheating.

Taxiing

3 Press the right rudder pedal to turn the airplane to the right and the left rudder pedal to turn to the left. It is recommended that you taxi no faster than a brisk walk. In a confined area, taxi at a speed slow enough to enable you to stop by reducing the power or shutting down the engine in the event of a brake failure.

Since the brakes can be controlled separately, applying the brakes in the direction of a turn can be helpful in reducing the radius of the turn. You can activate the left brake by pressing the top of the left rudder pedal and the right brake by pressing the top of the right rudder pedal.

Taxiing In Headwinds

While taxiing in moderate or strong wind conditions, you must use special techniques to maintain aircraft control. The aileron, rudder, and elevator (or stabilator) controls are relatively ineffective at slow speeds. However, as the speed of air over the control surfaces increases, control effectiveness also increases. The flight controls respond the same, whether you are taxiing at 5 knots with no wind or sitting still with a 5-knot headwind. However, if you taxi the airplane at 15 knots into a 15-knot wind, the controls have a 30-knot airflow over them and respond to that velocity of airflow.

1 Hold the yoke to maintain the ailerons in a neutral or level position.

When taxiing directly into a headwind there is little or no tendency for the airplane to tip since the wind flows over and under both wings equally.

2 Hold the yoke neutral or slightly forward to maintain the elevator (or stabilator) in a neutral or slightly down position. This will exert normal pressure on the nose gear.

Holding too much forward pressure on the yoke while taxing into a strong headwind forces the tail up and the nose down. This increases the load placed on the nose gear, compresses the nose strut, and puts the propeller closer to the ground. While this normally does not create a hazard, on rough or uneven terrain the likelihood of a propeller strike is increased.

3 When taxiing over rough ground, hold the yoke aft so the elevator (or stabilator) is raised. This procedure forces the tail down and increases propeller clearance.

Taxiing

Quartering Headwinds

In a strong quartering headwind, there is a tendency for the wind to get under the upwind wing and tip the airplane toward the downwind side. With improper aileron placement, the upwind wing can be lifted which can cause directional control problems or even overturn the airplane. In addition, wind striking the rudder can cause the airplane to turn into the wind. Improper elevator (or stabilator) position can reduce nosewheel friction and increase this weathervaning tendency.

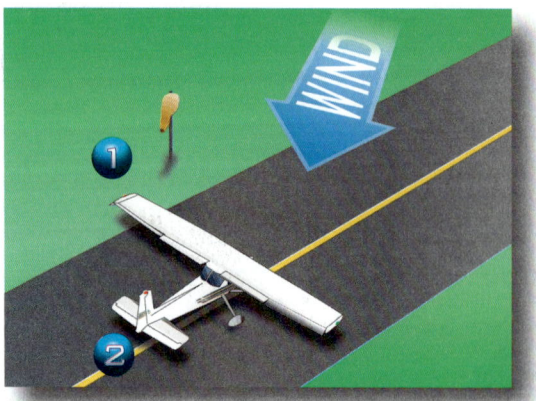

 Fully turn the yoke in the direction of the wind placing the upwind aileron in the up position. Due to reduced control effectiveness at slow taxi speeds, full aileron deflection is required.

 Hold the yoke to maintain the elevator (or stabilator) in a neutral or level position. A neutral elevator position will help maintain sufficient nosewheel friction and allow positive directional control.

Taxiing in Tailwinds

The effectiveness of the airplane controls also is influenced by tailwinds. For example, if you taxi the airplane at 5 knots with a tailwind of 5 knots, the taxi speed and the wind speed are canceled, and the controls respond as though no wind exists. If you slow the airplane, the controls respond as though there were an increasing tailwind component. When you stop the airplane completely, the control surfaces are subjected to the direct effects of a 5-knot tailwind.

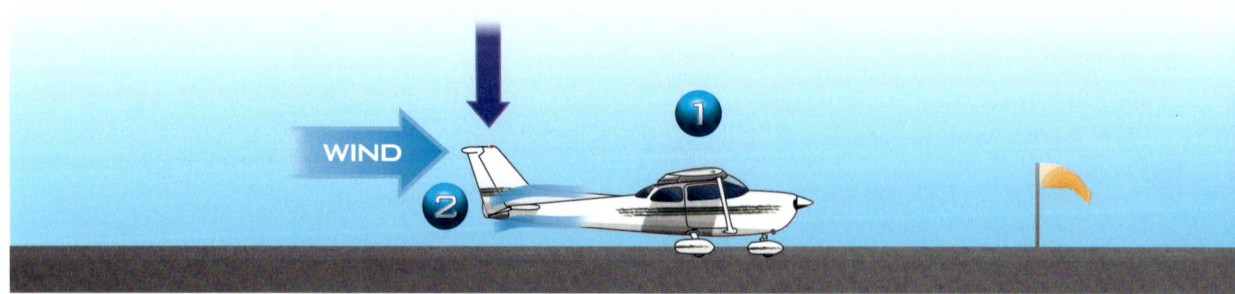

 Hold the yoke to maintain the ailerons in a neutral or level position.

In a strong tailwind you may need to reduce the throttle to idle to control your taxi speed. Taxiing in a tailwind usually requires less engine power because the wind has a tendency to push the airplane, increasing taxi speed.

 Hold the yoke full forward to maintain the elevator (or stabilator) in a full down position. This causes the wind to strike the upper surface of the elevator (or stabilator) and to exert a downward force on the tail.

If the elevator (or stabilator) is incorrectly positioned upward, the wind may raise the tail causing the airplane to have a tendency to tip or nose over.

QUARTERING TAILWINDS

A quartering tailwind is the most critical wind condition for taxiing a tricycle gear, high-wing airplane. Since quartering tailwinds have a tendency to flow beneath the elevator (or stabilator) and lift the tail, the airplane may tip over on the nosewheel and one main wheel.

1. Fully turn the yoke in the direction away from the wind. In a right quartering tailwind turn the yoke fully to the left, or left aileron up. Reverse the position of the aileron control when taxiing with a left quartering tailwind.

2. Hold the yoke full forward to maintain the elevator (or stabilator) in a down position which will counteract the airplane's tipping tendency.

Be particularly cautious when you are slowing down and beginning a turn in a quartering tailwind. The increasing tailwind component, combined with the normal tendency of the airplane to tip during the turn, makes the airplane especially vulnerable to being overturned. Slow taxi speeds and slow turns minimize this danger.

TAXIING

To meet the PTS requirements, you must:

- Exhibit knowledge of the elements related to safe taxi procedures.

- Perform a brake check immediately after the airplane begins moving.

- Position the flight controls properly for the existing wind conditions.

- Control direction and speed without excessive use of brakes.

- Comply with airport/taxiway markings, signals, ATC clearances, and instructions.

- Taxi so as to avoid other aircraft and hazards.

4 — BEFORE TAKEOFF CHECK

The before takeoff check is an integral part of every flight. When performing the before takeoff check, you should use the checklist provided by the airplane manufacturer or operator. This helps ensure that each item is checked in the proper sequence and that no items are omitted. After taxiing to the runup area, position the airplane so the propeller blast is not directed toward other aircraft, buildings, or vehicles. If possible, point the nose of the airplane into the wind to improve engine cooling. To prevent damage to the propeller and other parts of the airplane, avoid engine runups on loose gravel or sand. During the before takeoff check, you should divide your attention between your cockpit duties and outside the airplane. The before takeoff check may include, but is not limited to the following items.

1. Set the parking brake.

2. Verify that the cabin doors are securely closed and locked.

> Check to ensure that passengers who are sitting by doors know how to operate the latch and locking mechanism.

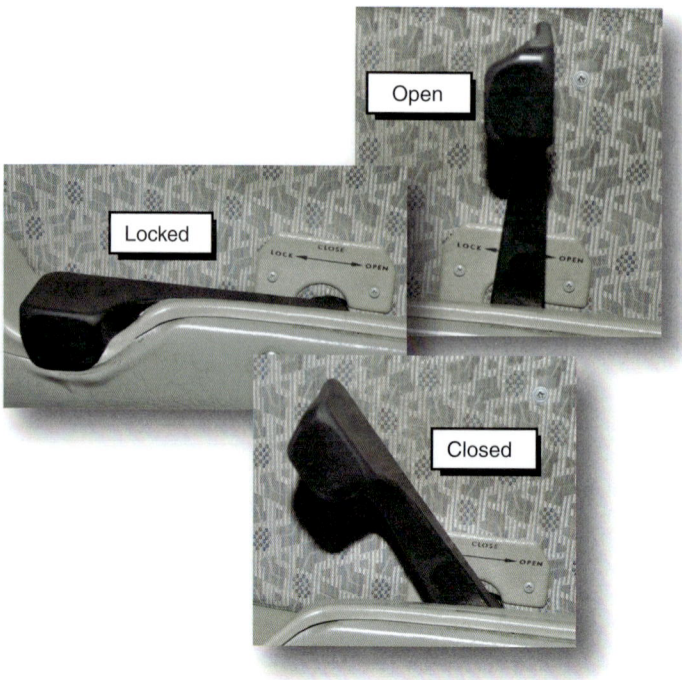

3. Check the flight controls for freedom of movement, full travel, and correct control surface deflection.

BEFORE TAKEOFF CHECK

4. Check and set the flight instruments.

   - Verify the airspeed indicator reads zero.
   - The attitude indicator should be erect with the miniature airplane aligned with the horizon.
   - Set the altimeter to the current altimeter setting or to the correct field elevation. If the altimeter does not indicate the field elevation within 75 feet, you should consider postponing the flight.
   - The miniature airplane in the turn coordinator should be level and the ball in the inclinometer centered.
   - Set the heading indicator to coincide with the magnetic compass.
   - Check that the vertical speed indicator (VSI) is pointing at zero. If the VSI is not pointing at zero, you may fly the aircraft and use the indicated value as the zero indication.

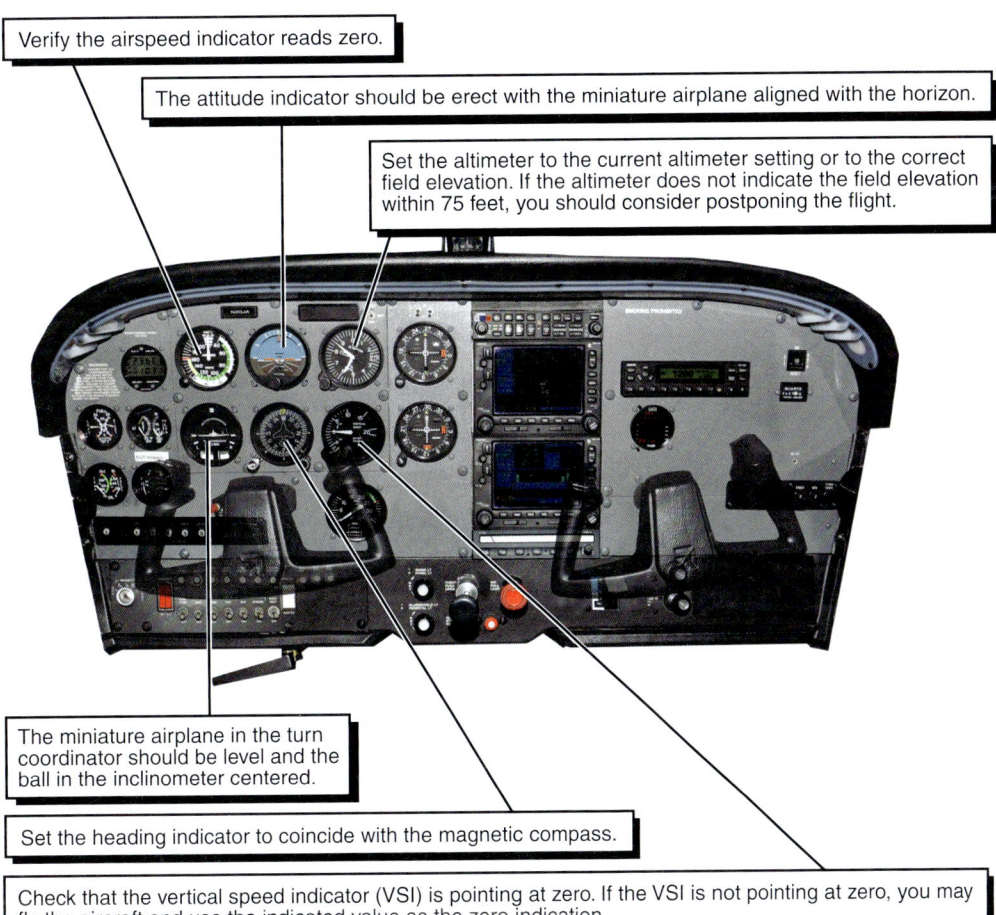

5. Position the fuel selector valve to the fullest tank or to the BOTH position, as recommended by the POH.

6. Set the mixture control to RICH as required for field elevation or as required by the POH.

   At high altitude airports, you may need to lean the mixture for smooth engine operations. Refer to the POH for the appropriate procedures.

7. Set the elevator trim and rudder trim (if installed) to the TAKEOFF position.

Before Takeoff Check

8. Smoothly add power to the r.p.m. setting recommended by the manufacturer for the power check (also called the runup). You should also hold the brakes to ensure the airplane does not move forward during the runup.

9. Check each magneto for proper operation. Test the magnetos by noting the r.p.m. with the magneto switch in the BOTH position, then move the magneto switch to the RIGHT position and note the r.p.m. drop. Next, return the magneto switch to BOTH, then switch to the LEFT position and again note the r.p.m. drop. Finally, return the magneto switch to the BOTH position for takeoff. The airplane manufacturer specifies the maximum permissible r.p.m. reductions for each magneto, as well as the maximum differential.

10. Position the carburetor heat control to ON and check for a corresponding drop in r.p.m., then return it to the COLD position. In some atmospheric conditions, carburetor ice may form while taxiing. This may be noted by a larger initial drop in r.p.m. followed by a slight increase in r.p.m. The initial drop may be accompanied by engine roughness which subsides with the r.p.m. increase.

11. Check the engine instruments and ammeter for normal indications. With the exception of the oil temperature gauge, the engine instruments should register in the green arcs. In cold weather, oil temperature might not indicate in the normal range until after takeoff. An ammeter discharge or low voltage light may indicate a faulty alternator, broken alternator belt, or excessive electrical load.

Before Takeoff Check

12. Check the suction gauge for a normal indication. A low reading may indicate a dirty air filter. Unreliable gyro indications may result if sufficient suction is not maintained.

13. Reduce power to approximately 1,000 r.p.m.

14. Set the communication and navigation radios to the appropriate frequencies.

15. Set the transponder to the appropriate code. While you typically should use the code 1200 for VFR flight, you may be assigned a discrete transponder code at some airports.

16. Ensure your landing light, navigation lights, flashing beacon and/or strobe lights are on as required.

17. Adjust the throttle friction as desired.

18. Review performance airspeeds.

19. Release the parking brake.

20. Clear the area of traffic before taxiing into the takeoff position. After receiving your takeoff clearance (if required), you should check the final approach path, any taxiways you may cross to get to the runway, and the runway itself.

BEFORE TAKEOFF CHECK

To meet the PTS requirements, you must:

- Exhibit knowledge of the elements related to the before takeoff check. This shall include the reasons for checking each item and how to detect malfunctions.

- Position the airplane properly considering other aircraft/vessels, wind and surface conditions.

- Divide attention inside and outside the cockpit.

- Ensure that engine temperature and pressure are suitable for run-up and takeoff.

- Accomplish the before takeoff checklist and ensures the airplane is in safe operating condition.

- Review takeoff performance airspeeds, takeoff distances, departure, and emergency procedures.

- Avoid runway incursions and/or ensure no conflict with traffic prior to taxiing into takeoff position.

5 — Postflight Procedures

Many pilots maintain a high level of vigilance throughout a flight; however, the flight is not over once you arrive on the runway — you still have several important tasks to perform as part of your postflight procedures. These tasks include completing the after landing and engine shutdown checklists as well as parking and securing the airplane.

After Landing

After landing, gradually slow the airplane to normal taxi speed before turning off the runway. You should use the manufacturer's checklist to perform the after landing check once the airplane is stopped clear of the active runway.

1. Retract the wing flaps.

2. **Non-fuel-injected**—Move the carburetor heat control to the COLD position to prevent unfiltered air from being drawn into the carburetor, causing damage to the internal components of the engine.

3. At tower controlled airports, contact ground control for taxi clearance.

4. After receiving your taxi clearance, clear the area around the airplane to avoid taxi conflicts. While taxiing, you should position the flight controls as appropriate for the prevailing wind conditions.

Postflight Procedures

Parking and Securing

When taxiing into the parking area, you should use a safe taxi speed and follow any hand signals you receive from ramp personnel. In general, there are two ways to park an airplane. One way is to taxi the airplane into its designated parking spot, shut down and secure the engine, then safely deplane any passengers. However, because of the proximity of other aircraft, this procedure may not be possible. In this situation, you should taxi the airplane near your intended parking spot and position the airplane so that the propwash does not endanger people or property on the ramp. Then, shut down and secure the engine, safely deplane any passengers, and use a towbar to maneuver the airplane into parking. Once you have positioned the airplane in its parking spot, you should tie down the airplane and perform a postflight inspection.

Engine Shutdown

Many aircraft have specific procedures for engine shutdown. You should always follow the recommendations contained in the POH.

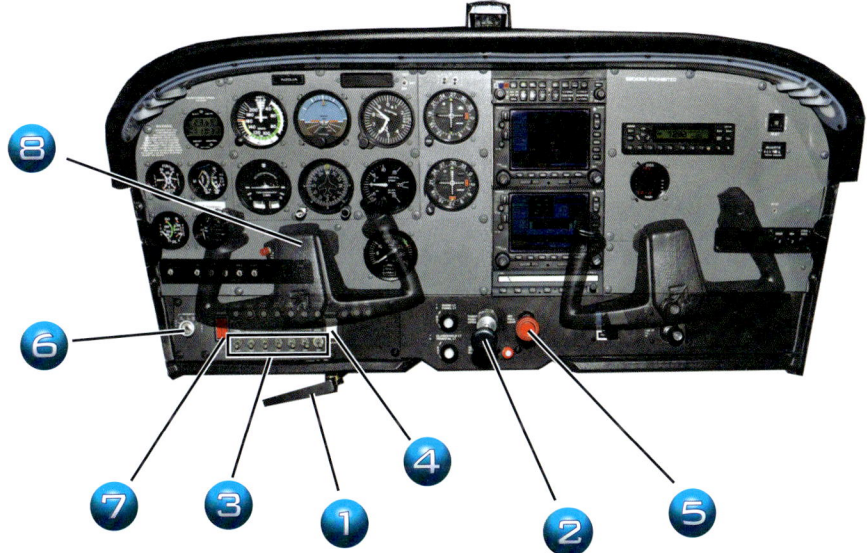

1. Set the parking brake.

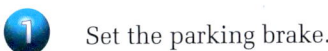

At this point, you may wish to check for accidental activation of the ELT by tuning 121.5 MHz on a communication radio.

2. Set the throttle to idle, or as recommended by the manufacturer.

3. Turn OFF all electrical equipment.

4. Turn OFF the avionics power switch.

5. Set the mixture control to IDLE CUT-OFF.

6. Turn the ignition switch OFF when the engine stops. As an added precaution, remove the key from the ignition.

7. Turn the master switch OFF.

8. Install the control lock.

Postflight Procedures

TIEDOWN

To avoid damage from high winds or gusty conditions, you must secure the airplane properly. This is usually accomplished using chocks and tiedown ropes or chains.

1. Release the parking brake and position the airplane in the parking spot using a towbar, if necessary.

> If a towbar is not available, you can move the airplane by pushing on various components. You can push on the leading edge of the horizontal and vertical stabilizers as long as you only apply pressure to the leading edge near the fuselage. The leading edge of the wing also is a good push point on low-wing airplanes; however, be careful to only apply pressure at rib locations. On most high-wing airplanes, you can move the airplane by pushing on the wing struts.

2. Place chocks in front of and behind the main wheels.

3. Secure the airplane with tiedown chains or ropes.

4. Install the pitot tube cover.

5. Complete a postflight inspection using a checklist, if available. A typical postflight inspection includes checking for leaking fluids, airframe damage, proper tire inflation, and a variety of other items.

Postflight Procedures

6. Remove all personal materials from the cockpit, stow the seatbelts, and close and lock all doors and windows.

 **AFTER LANDING, PARKING AND SECURING**

To meet the PTS requirements, you must:

- Exhibit knowledge of the elements related to after landing, parking, and securing procedures.

- Maintain directional control after touchdown while decelerating to an appropriate speed.

- Observe runway hold lines and other surface control markings and lighting.

- Park in an appropriate area, considering the safety of nearby persons and property.

- Follow the appropriate procedure for engine shutdown.

- Complete the appropriate checklist.

- Conduct an appropriate postflight inspection and secures the aircraft.

EXERCISES — GROUND OPERATIONS

EXERCISES — GROUND OPERATIONS

1 — PREFLIGHT INSPECTION

1. What should you use to ensure that all steps are completed when performing a preflight inspection? *Refere to and follow the aircraft specific checklist.*

2. What documents are required on board the airplane? *Airworthiness, Registration, Radio class POH, weight, balance info*

3. How can you tell when water is present in a fuel sample? *Water will sink to the bottom of the sample cup and seperate.*

4. True/False. Nicks on the propeller can cause excessive stress and should be checked by a certificated mechanic. *True*

5. What documents are not required to be on board the airplane? _____
    A. Airworthiness certificate, aircraft logbooks
    (B.) Airworthiness directives (ADs), maintenance records
    C. Airworthiness directives (ADs), approved flight manual

2 — ENGINE STARTING

1. True/False. Before you start the engine, a thorough look around the propeller eliminates the need for opening a window or door and shouting "*CLEAR!*" *False*

2. ✗ The primer pumps fuel into what part of the engine? ~~Carburator~~ *Engine cylinders*

3. Where would you find procedural information on starting the airplane with an external power source? *Pilots Operating Handbook*

4. After you start the engine in cold weather, the oil pressure should register properly within how many seconds? *60*

5. After starting the engine, what action should you take in the event the oil pressure does not register within the green arc in the recommended time? *Shut off the master switch.*

3 — TAXIING

The following questions pertain to a tricycle gear airplane.

1. True/False. Taxi speed is primarily controlled by using the brakes. *False*

2. Does the effectiveness of the aileron, rudder, and elevator (or stabilator) controls increase or decrease as the airplane's speed decreases? *Decreases*

Exercises – Ground Operations

3. What action is helpful in reducing the radius of a turn while taxiing?
   lightly applying the inside brake.

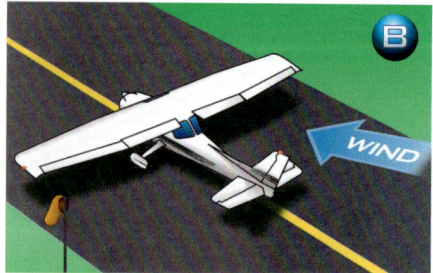

4. How would you position the flight controls for the surface wind conditions depicted in illustration A?
   Yoke left to raise the upwing aileron and elevator neutral

5. How would you position the flight controls for the surface wind conditions depicted in illustration B?
   Yoke left and Forward

4 — Before Takeoff Check

1. Why should you position the nose of the airplane into the wind during the runup?
   To improve engine cooling

2. True/False. If the altimeter setting is not available during the before takeoff check, you can adjust the altimeter to agree with field elevation. _True_

3. As you apply carburetor heat during the runup should the r.p.m. increase or decrease (assuming no carburetor ice exists)? _Decrease_

4. What may occur if sufficient vacuum pressure (suction) is not maintained?
   Attitude and Heading Indicators may malfunction and poor engine perform

5. True/False. Unless you are assigned a discrete transponder code, you should use 1220 for VFR flight. _True_

5 — Postflight Procedures

1. **Non-fuel-injected**—Why should you ensure the carburetor heat is COLD while taxiing?
   To prevent unfiltered air particals from entering the engine

2. How can you check for accidental activation of your ELT?
   Tune to 121.5

3. True/False. You should install the control lock before engine shutdown. _False_

4. If you move an airplane by pushing on the leading edge of a wing, where should you apply pressure?
   near the root / cockpit

5. While securing your airplane, where should you normally place the chocks?
   Infrontof and Behind the main gear wheels

BASIC MANEUVERS

BASIC MANEUVERS

BASIC MANEUVERS

MANEUVER 6 2-2
 STRAIGHT-AND-LEVEL FLIGHT

MANEUVER 7 2-4
 CLIMBS

MANEUVER 8 2-6
 DESCENTS

MANEUVER 9 2-8
 TURNS

EXERCISES 2-13

Video Volume I — Ground Operations, Basic Maneuvers, Airport Operations, and Emergency Landing Procedures

Computer Training — Basic Maneuvers

6 — Straight-And-Level Flight

During straight-and-level flight you can maintain a constant heading and altitude by controlling the nose and wing positions with reference to the natural horizon. Although the flight instruments may be used as a cross-check to confirm that you are maintaining straight-and-level flight, your primary reference should be the horizon to the front and side of your airplane. Keeping your eyes primarily focused outside the cockpit also helps you see and avoid other aircraft.

Trim adjustments eliminate the need for continuous forward or backward pressure on the yoke to maintain attitude. If the airplane feels nose-heavy, you are holding back pressure to maintain a given attitude. Likewise, if forward pressure is required, the airplane will feel tail-heavy. When it is properly trimmed, you will not have to apply either forward or back pressure to maintain a constant pitch attitude. Use the trim tab only to remove pressure; do not use it to fly the airplane. The proper procedure is to set the airplane in the desired pitch attitude and at the selected airspeed, then trim away any control pressure necessary to hold that attitude. With a few exceptions, trim tab adjustments should be made whenever you must apply a continuous forward or rearward force to the yoke. The same principles apply to trimming the rudder however, since it is not as easy to feel the control pressures, you should refer to the turn coordinator while trimming the rudder to maintain coordinated flight.

When you are introduced to straight-and-level flight (or any other maneuver), your instructor will normally demonstrate the maneuver first, then pass the controls to you. To ensure that it is clear as to who has control of the airplane, the FAA strongly recommends the use of a three-step process when exchanging the flight controls. During the preflight briefing, you should review with your instructor the following procedures for passing control of the airplane.

PILOT **PASSING** CONTROL: *"You have the flight controls."*

PILOT **TAKING** CONTROL: *"I have the flight controls."*

PILOT **PASSING** CONTROL: *"You have the flight controls."*

| 090 Heading | Wings Level | 2000' Altitude | 080 Heading | Nose Low Attitude | 1800' Altitude |

Straight-And-Level Flight

The pilot passing the controls should continue to fly until the pilot taking the controls acknowledges the exchange by saying, *"I have the flight controls."* A visual check also is recommended to ensure that the other pilot actually has the controls. There may be times when your instructor desires to assume control of the airplane from you. If this is necessary, your instructor should take the controls while informing you, *"I have the flight controls."*

 Establish the airplane on a specfic heading and altitude. Adjust the rudder to maintain coordinated flight and trim to relieve control pressures.

- Maintain a wings-level position by keeping the wingtips a given distance above (high-wing airplane) or below (low-wing airplane) the horizon.
- By keeping a point on the airplane's nose or spot on the windshield in a constant position in relation to a point on the horizon, you can maintain your desired altitude.

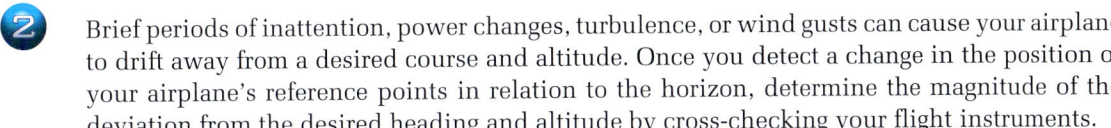 Brief periods of inattention, power changes, turbulence, or wind gusts can cause your airplane to drift away from a desired course and altitude. Once you detect a change in the position of your airplane's reference points in relation to the horizon, determine the magnitude of the deviation from the desired heading and altitude by cross-checking your flight instruments.

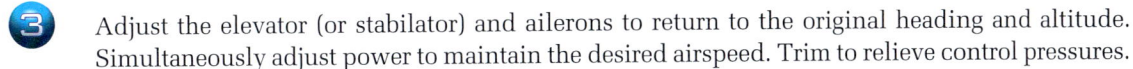 Adjust the elevator (or stabilator) and ailerons to return to the original heading and altitude. Simultaneously adjust power to maintain the desired airspeed. Trim to relieve control pressures.

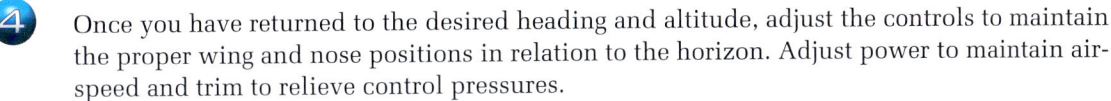 Once you have returned to the desired heading and altitude, adjust the controls to maintain the proper wing and nose positions in relation to the horizon. Adjust power to maintain airspeed and trim to relieve control pressures.

 **STRAIGHT-AND-LEVEL FLIGHT**
The PTS does not include specific criteria for straight-and-level flight using visual references. However, it does have performance standards for basic instrument straight-and-level flight. (See Maneuver #30.)

090 Heading   Wings Level   2000' Altitude

7 — CLIMBS

A climb is a basic maneuver designed to produce a gain in altitude. When practicing climbs, your objectives are to become proficient in establishing the proper climb attitude, applying the appropriate control pressure, and learning the trim technique necessary to maintain the climb attitude. During your training you will practice a variety of climbs; some will be constant-rate climbs and others will be constant-airspeed climbs. The most common types of climb speeds are:

- **Best angle-of-climb speed, V_X** — An airspeed that results in the greatest altitude gain in the shortest distance.

- **Best rate-of-climb speed, V_Y** — An airspeed that provides the most gain in altitude in the least amount of time.

- **Cruise climb speed** — An airspeed that is normally used during cross-country flight and results in a relatively higher groundspeed while climbing to cruising altitude.

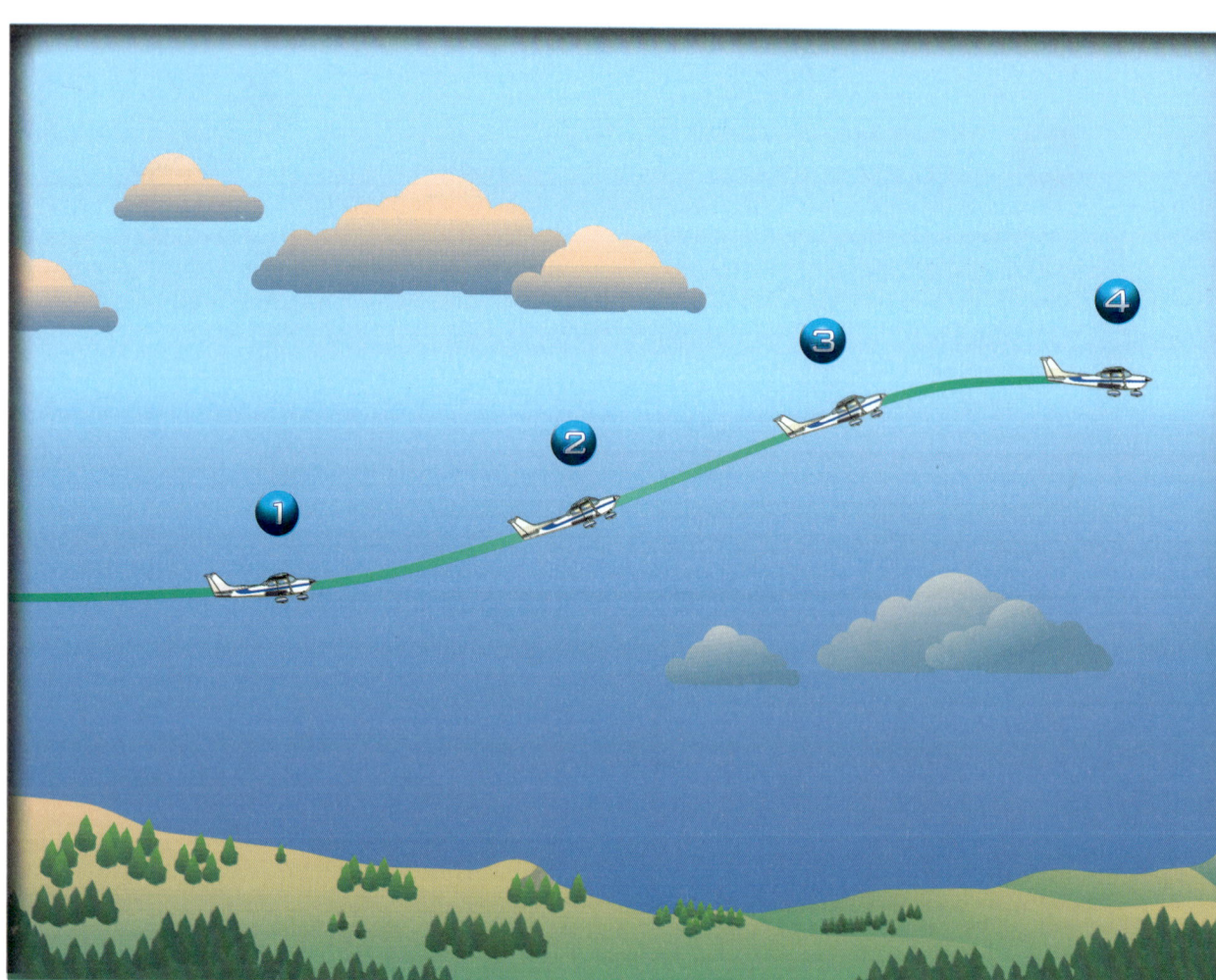

Climbs

 After clearing the airspace around your airplane, simultaneously add power and apply back pressure on the yoke. Add right rudder to compensate for the left-turning tendencies which result from the increase in pitch attitude and decrease in airspeed. Trim up elevator (or stabilator) and right rudder (if available).

 Maintain climb airspeed and heading using outside references and instrument cross-checks. Use changes in pitch attitude to maintain your airspeed and bank angle adjustments to correct for heading deviations. If changes are necessary, make small adjustments, allow the airplane to stabilize, then trim to relieve the control pressures.

 If you are climbing at 500 f.p.m., return to straight-and-level flight by gradually lowering the nose approximately 50 feet prior to the desired leveloff altitude. Maintain climb power to accelerate to cruise speed. As the airplane accelerates, less right rudder pressure will be needed (or increasing left rudder pressure against the right rudder trim) as the left-turning tendencies diminish.

Generally, a 10% lead is sufficient for leveloff. For example, 10% of a 500 f.p.m. climb would yield a 50-foot lead for leveloff.

 Reduce power to the cruise setting when the desired cruise speed is reached. Trim to relieve the control pressures and, if necessary, lean the mixture.

CLIMBS

The PTS does not include specific criteria for climbs using visual references. However, it does have performance standards for basic instrument constant-airspeed climbs. (See Maneuver #30.)

8 — DESCENTS

The descent is a basic flight maneuver which results in a loss of altitude without gaining excessive airspeed, controlling the rate of descent with pitch attitude and, in some cases, power. Initially, you will practice descents at the airspeed used for approaches to landings. After you learn this type of descent, you will practice the cruise descent which is flown at cruise airspeed and results in a higher groundspeed.

To find the specific airspeed corresponding to the type of descent you want to perform, you should refer to the POH for your airplane. When you perform a descent, you should develop the practice of establishing the proper flight attitudes using visual references first, then cross-check your parameters using the flight instruments.

1. After clearing the airspace around your airplane, apply carburetor heat (if applicable) and reduce power as required. Gradually apply back pressure to maintain altitude while the airplane slows to the descent airspeed.

2. When you reach the descent airspeed, lower the nose slightly to set the descent pitch attitude and maintain airspeed. Trim to relieve control pressures.

> In many aircraft, the descent attitude is nearly the same as that used for straight-and-level cruising flight. While you normally control a descent with power and/or pitch attitude changes, you can also use configuration changes. Extending the landing gear (if applicable) or flaps increases your descent rate without increasing your airspeed.

3. Maintain descent airspeed and heading. Cross-check your airspeed and rate of descent using the airplane nose position in relation to the horizon, the airspeed indicator, the vertical speed indicator, and the pitch attitude on the attitude indicator.

- In a power-off glide, pitch attitude controls airspeed; raise the nose to decrease airspeed, and lower the nose to increase airspeed. Always trim after any adjustment is made to pitch attitude.

DESCENTS

- To maintain a constant airspeed in a powered descent, you will need to adjust the nose attitude when you change power. A power addition requires a slightly higher nose attitude, while a slightly lower nose attitude is needed for a power reduction. Always trim after any adjustment is made to pitch attitude or power.

- To maintain heading, refer to the position of each wingtip in relation to the horizon and cross-check using the heading indicator. Also, check the turn coordinator to ensure you maintain coordinated flight. If changes are necessary, make small adjustments, allow the airplane to stabilize again, then trim to relieve the control pressures.

 If you are descending at 500 f.p.m., return to straight-and-level flight by gradually raising the nose approximately 50 feet prior to the desired leveloff altitude. Add power to maintain airspeed.

Generally, a 10% lead is sufficient for leveloff. For example, 10% of a 500 f.p.m. climb would yield a 50-foot lead for leveloff.

 Once the airplane is stabilized in straight-and-level cruising flight, trim to relieve control pressures. Set the carburetor heat to COLD (if applicable) and, if necessary, enrichen the mixture.

 **DESCENTS**

The PTS does not include specific criteria for descents using visual references. However, it does have performance standards for basic instrument constant airspeed descents. (See Maneuver #30.)

9 — Turns

Turns are accomplished by using outside visual references and monitoring the flight instruments. You will normally begin by practicing level turns and, once mastered, move on to climbing and descending turns. Turns are divided into three classes:

- **Shallow turn** — A turn of less than approximately 20° angle of bank

- **Medium turn** — A turn between approximately 20° to 45° angle of bank

- **Steep turn** — A turn of approximately 45° angle of bank or more

Level Turns

When you make turns by visual reference, the nose of the airplane appears to move in an arc with respect to the horizon. You can determine when you have reached the proper angle of bank by observing the angle of the cowling and instrument panel with respect to the horizon.

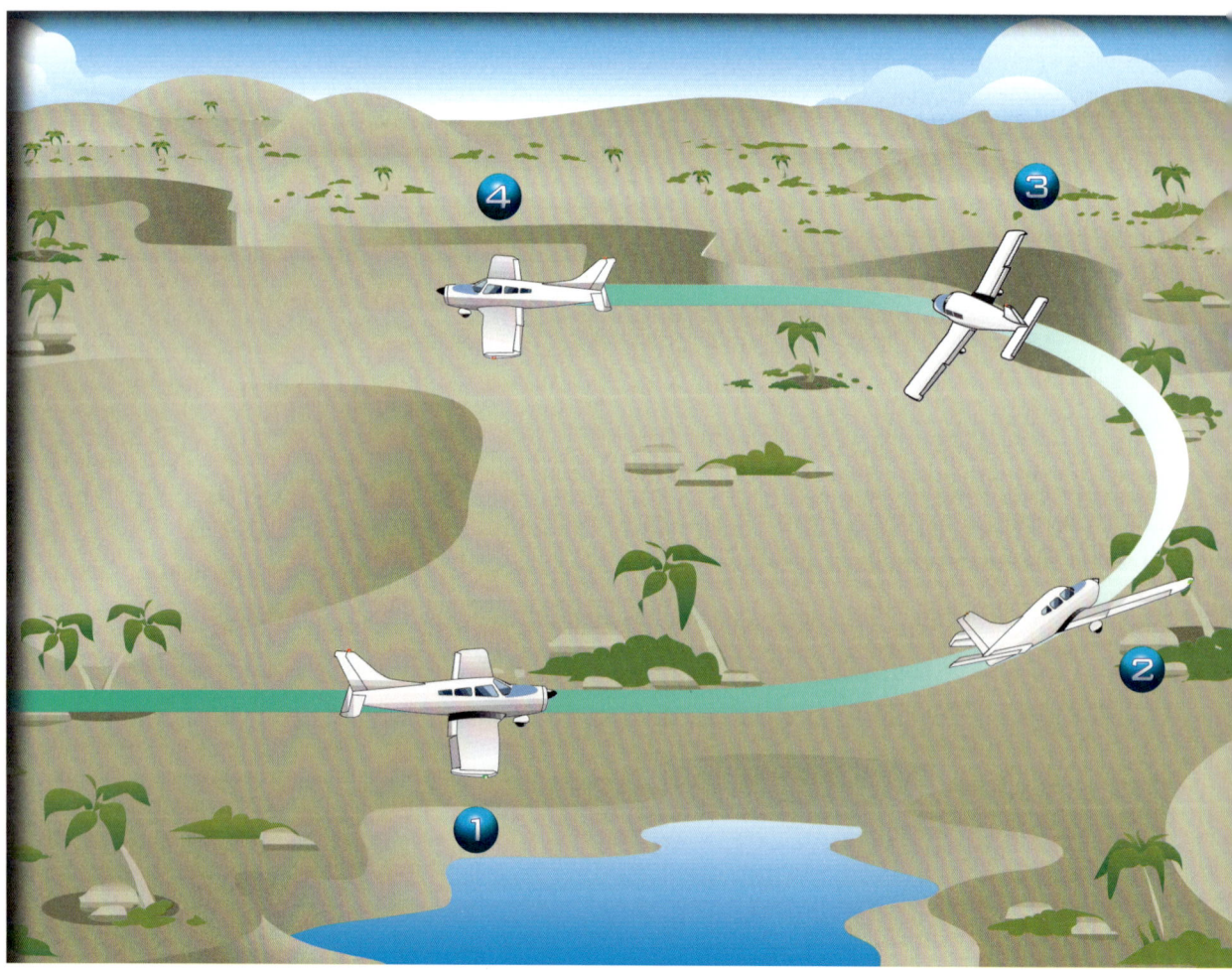

TURNS

1. After clearing the airspace around your airplane, add power slightly, turn the airplane in the desired direction, and apply a slight amount of back pressure on the yoke to maintain altitude. Maintain coordinated flight by applying rudder in the direction of the turn.

> The ailerons control the roll rate, as well as the angle of bank. The rate at which the airplane rolls depends on how much aileron deflection you use. How far the airplane rolls (steepness of the bank) depends on how long you deflect the ailerons, since the airplane continues to roll as long as the ailerons are deflected.

2. When you reach the desired angle of bank, neutralize the ailerons. Trim to relieve control pressures.

3. Lead the roll-out by approximately one-half your angle of bank. Use coordinated aileron and rudder control pressures as you roll out. Simultaneously, begin releasing the back pressure on the yoke so aileron, rudder, and elevator (or stabilator) pressures are neutralized when the airplane reaches the wings-level position.

> Leading your roll-out heading by one-half your bank angle is a good rule of thumb for initial training. However, keep in mind that the required amount of lead really depends on the type of turn, turn rate, and rollout rate. As you gain experience, you will develop a consistent roll-in and roll-out technique for various types of turns.

4. Upon reaching a wings-level attitude, reduce power and trim to remove control pressures.

LEVEL TURNS

The PTS does not include specific criteria for level turns using visual references. However, it does have performance standards for basic instrument turns to headings. (See Maneuver #30.)

CLIMBING TURNS

The objective of practicing climbing turns is to smoothly combine the techniques of climbs with those of turns. Initially, you may practice climbing turns with a two-step process. First, you establish climb power and attitude, then roll to the desired angle of bank. As you gain experience and proficiency, you will enter the maneuver by establishing both the climb and bank attitude at the same time.

You should use the same airspeed for straight climbs and climbing turns. However, your rate of climb will be less for climbing turns than straight climbs. Generally, you perform climbing turns using shallow bank angles, because steep bank angles divert more of the vertical component of lift, which causes a reduction in rate of climb.

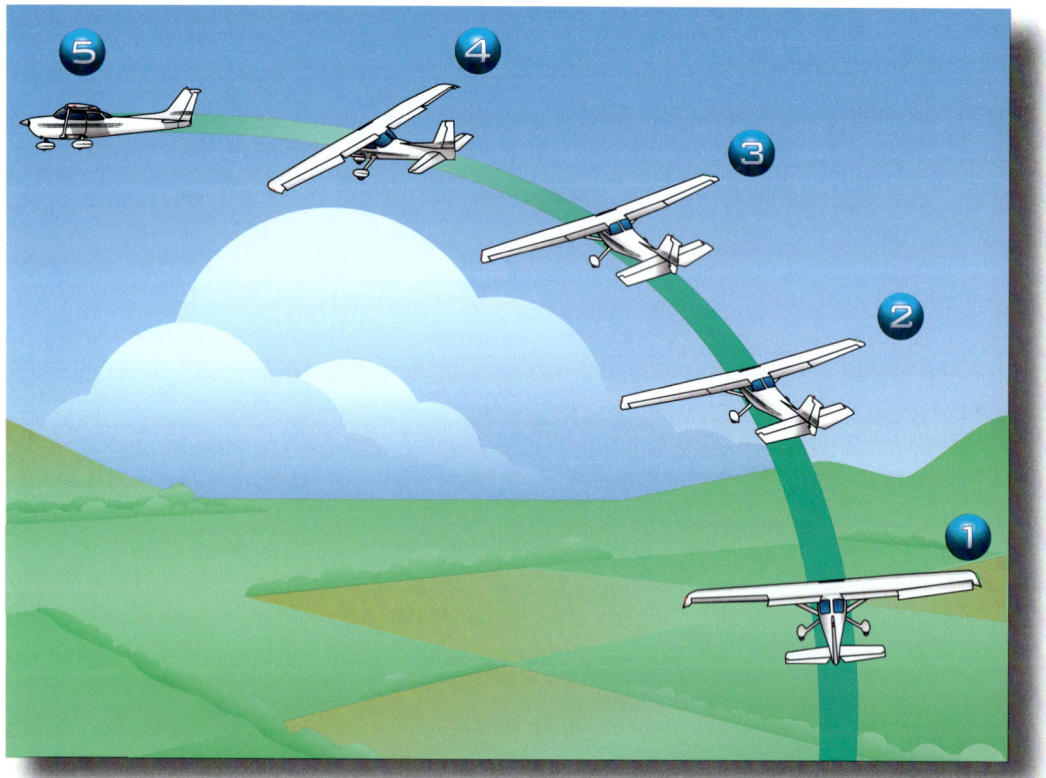

1. After clearing the airspace around your airplane, simultaneously add power, apply back pressure on the yoke and turn the airplane in the desired direction with coordinated aileron and rudder control input.

2. When you reach the desired angle of bank, neutralize the ailerons. Trim to relieve control pressures.

3. Maintain the desired climb airspeed and angle of bank using outside references, periodically cross-checking your flight instruments.

4. Lead the roll-out by approximately one-half your angle of bank. Use coordinated aileron and rudder control pressures as you roll out. Simultaneously, begin releasing the back pressure on the yoke so aileron, rudder, and elevator (or stabilator) pressures are neutralized when the airplane reaches the desired heading and altitude.

TURNS

You rarely reach the desired altitude and heading at the same time. If you reach the heading first, level the wings and maintain the climb until you reach the desired altitude. If you reach the altitude first, lower the nose to maintain the desired altitude and continue the turn toward the desired heading. If you reach both the desired altitude and heading at the same time, you can perform these procedures simultaneously.

 Once the desired cruise airspeed has been obtained, reduce power, trim to relieve control pressures, and lean the mixture (if necessary).

CLIMBING TURNS
The PTS does not include specific criteria for climbing turns using visual references. However, it does have performance standards for basic instrument constant airspeed climbs and turns to headings. (See Maneuver #30.)

DESCENDING TURNS

Descending turns to preselected headings and altitudes combine the procedures for straight descents with those used in turns. As with climbing turns, you may practice descending turns using a two-step process. First, you establish the descent attitude, then roll to the desired angle of bank. As you gain proficiency, you will learn to establish the descent attitude and bank simultaneously.

Maintain the same airspeed in descending turns as in straight descents. However, your rate of descent will be higher in a descending turn than in a straight descent with a comparable power setting because the vertical lift component is less when the airplane banks. You can compensate for this with a slight addition of power over what is used in a straight descent.

TURNS

 After clearing the airspace around your airplane, apply carburetor heat (if applicable), reduce power, and lower the nose. Simultaneously, turn toward the desired heading using coordinated aileron and rudder application.

 When you reach the desired angle of bank, neutralize the ailerons. Trim to relieve control pressures.

 Maintain the desired descent airspeed and angle of bank using outside references, periodically cross-checking your flight instruments.

> Use power to control the rate of descent. Make the initial power setting for the desired rate of descent and allow the pitch attitude and the rate of descent to stabilize. If you desire a higher rate of descent, reduce power. In contrast, add power if you desire a lower rate of descent.

 Lead the roll-out by approximately one-half your angle of bank. Use coordinated aileron and rudder control pressures as your roll out. Simultaneously, add power to the cruise setting and adjust the nose position so aileron, rudder, and elevator (or stabilator) pressures are neutralized when the airplane reaches the desired heading and altitude.

 Set the carburetor heat to the COLD position, trim to relieve control pressures, and, if necessary, enrichen the mixture.

DESCENDING TURNS

The PTS does not include specific criteria for descending turns using visual references. However, it does have performance standards for basic instrument constant airspeed descents and turns to headings. (See Maneuver #30.)

EXERCISES — BASIC MANEUVERS

6 — STRAIGHT-AND-LEVEL FLIGHT

1. During straight-and-level flight, what is the primary visual reference used for maintaining altitude and heading?

2. What is a safety-related advantage of keeping your eyes primarily focused outside the cockpit?

3. True/False. To maintain straight-and-level flight, you normally need to make a continuous series of small adjustments in pitch and bank. _____

4. What is the primary reason for making trim adjustments? _____
    A. To correct heading
    B. To change pitch attitude
    C. To relieve control pressures

5. How can you determine the magnitude of a deviation from your desired heading and altitude?

7 — CLIMBS

1. Which type of climb speed results in the greatest gain in altitude in the shortest distance?

2. Which type of climb speed provides the most gain in altitude in the least amount of time?

3. True/False. As the pitch attitude is increased and the airspeed decreases, left-turning tendencies become less pronounced. _____

4. Would you expect a need for a decrease or increase of right rudder pressure as the aircraft accelerates during leveloff?

5. What percentage of your vertical speed is normally used to determine the lead for leveloff? _____

EXERCISES — BASIC MANEUVERS

8 — DESCENTS

1. True/False. You can control your rate of descent with pitch attitude. _____

2. Will a cruise descent result in a higher or lower groundspeed than a typical descent used for approach to landing?

3. During a 500 f.p.m. descent, you have been instructed to level off at 4,000 feet MSL. What altitude should you begin your leveloff?

4. True/False. You can decrease your descent rate by lowering the flaps. _____

5. Would a power increase during a constant airspeed, power-on descent require you to raise or lower the nose to maintain airspeed?

9 — TURNS

1. Turns are divided into three classes or types. What are the classes of turns and how many degrees of bank are associated with each?

2. True/False. During a level turn, you maintain the same amount of aileron deflection throughout the turn. _____

3. What determines how far an airplane rolls?

4. You are in a climbing turn to the right, using a 30° angle of bank, and have been directed to rollout on a heading of 090°. On what heading should you begin your rollout?

5. How can you compensate for the increased rate of descent you experience in a descending turn, as opposed to a straight descent?

AIRPORT OPERATIONS

AIRPORT OPERATIONS

AIRPORT OPERATIONS

MANEUVER 10 3-2
　NORMAL TAKEOFF AND CLIMB

MANEUVER 11 3-4
　CROSSWIND TAKEOFF AND CLIMB

MANEUVER 12 3-6
　TRAFFIC PATTERNS

MANEUVER 13 3-12
　NORMAL APPROACH AND LANDING

MANEUVER 14 3-20
　CROSSWIND APPROACH AND LANDING

EXERCISES............................... 3-23

Video Volume I — Ground Operations, Basic Maneuvers, Airport Operations, and Emergency Landing Procedures

Computer Training — Airport Operations

10 — Normal Takeoff and Climb

Each takeoff is affected by the wind conditions, runway surface and length, and possible obstructions at the end of the runway. The takeoff procedures outlined here are provided as general guidelines only. Be sure to consult your airplane's POH for the proper checklists and procedures.

1. Complete the before takeoff check. With the exception of the oil temperature gauge, all engine instruments must register within the normal operating range prior to takeoff.

2. Ensure that the runway, as well as the approach and departure paths are clear of other aircraft.
   - At an uncontrolled airport, broadcast your intentions for departure on the common traffic advisory frequency (CTAF).
   - At a controlled airport, contact the tower and inform them you are ready for departure. You must obtain a clearance from the control tower prior to taxiing onto the runway, and prior to takeoff.

3. Taxi onto the runway, line up with the runway centerline, center the nosewheel, and neutralize the ailerons. Check the windsock to determine the wind position in relation to the runway and then begin the takeoff roll.
   - Advance the throttle smoothly to takeoff power, and as the airplane starts to roll, select a point on the cowl through which the centerline of the runway passes and use it as a reference point for directional control. Apply right rudder to counteract engine torque.

> An abrupt application of power may cause the airplane to yaw sharply to the left due to the torque effects of the engine and propeller. Keep your hand on the throttle throughout the takeoff to ensure that it does not slide back during the takeoff roll. This also allows you to close the throttle quickly if you decide to abort the takeoff.

   - Check the engine instruments to ensure the engine is developing full power and is functioning within its operational limits. Slow acceleration or any hesitation in power is sufficient reason to discontinue the takeoff.

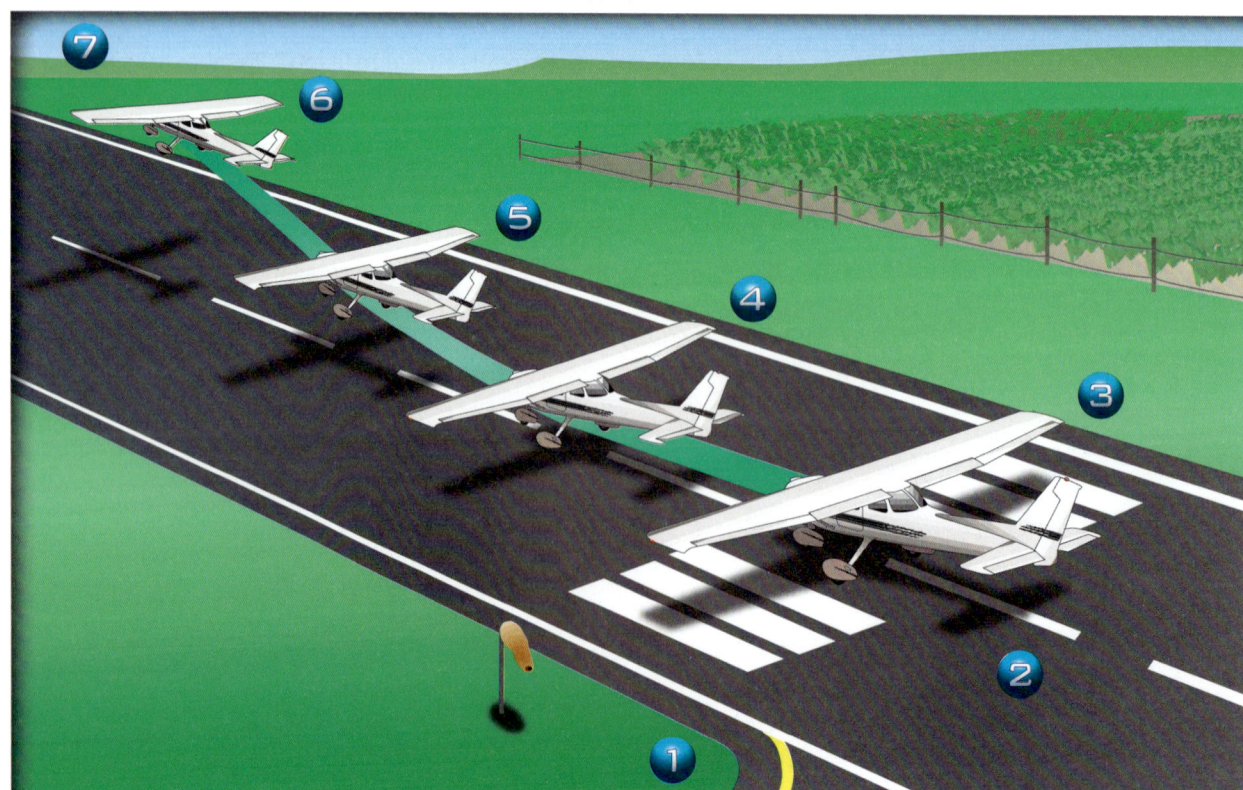

NORMAL TAKEOFF AND CLIMB

- Maintain directional control with the rudder pedals and use a neutral aileron position if the wind is aligned with the runway.

So there is no tendency to press the brakes inadvertently, rest your feet on the floor with the balls of your feet on the bottom edges of the rudder pedals.

 4. As speed increases and the controls become more effective, reduce rudder pressure to maintain directional control and apply slight back pressure to the yoke.

 5. Establish the takeoff attitude at the speed recommended by the manufacturer. As the airplane lifts off the runway, note the nose position in relation to the horizon and then maintain this attitude by using elevator (or stabilator) pressure.

The takeoff attitude is important since it is a compromise between holding the nose on the ground and selecting an attitude which is too nose high. If the nosewheel is held on the ground too long, the airplane tends to build excess airspeed, which increases the takeoff distance. With an excessively nose-high attitude, the airplane may be forced into the air prematurely and then settle back to the runway. Also, the airplane may be at such a high angle of attack (high drag condition) that it cannot accelerate to climb speed.

 6. Accelerate to the climb speed recommended by the manufacturer and adjust the pitch attitude to maintain the climb speed. Fly the departure leg of the traffic pattern straight out on an extension of the runway centerline. Use right rudder to counteract the airplane's left-turning tendency.

The initial climb speed varies with the airplane flap position and local conditions, such as the presence of obstacles in the departure path. You may need to fly at the obstacle clearance speed, best angle-of-climb speed (V_X), or best rate-of-climb speed (V_Y), as specified in the POH.

 7. Once you have reached a safe altitude, adjust the power to the recommended climb setting and trim to relieve any control pressures. Complete the appropriate checklist procedures, and depart or remain in the traffic pattern.

If a control tower is in operation, you can request and usually receive approval for any type of departure. The standard procedure for departing an uncontrolled airport is to fly straight out or to make a 45° turn in the direction of the traffic pattern.

TAKEOFF EMERGENCIES

Although an engine malfunction on takeoff is rare, the possibility does exist. If you experience a power loss on the takeoff roll, abort the takeoff quickly by moving the throttle to the idle position. Use the rudder to maintain directional control and the brakes as necessary to stop the airplane. If the engine malfunction occurs just after liftoff, you should reduce the pitch attitude slightly and allow the airplane to settle back to the runway. If sufficient runway does not exist, and you have not yet attained a safe maneuvering altitude, you have no choice but to land straight ahead. In this situation, you should make only small heading changes to avoid obstacles and should not attempt to turn back to the runway.

NORMAL TAKEOFF AND CLIMB

To meet the PTS requirements, you must:

- Exhibit knowledge of the elements related to a normal and crosswind takeoff, climb operations, and rejected takeoff procedures.
- Position the flight controls for the existing wind conditions.
- Clear the area; taxies into the takeoff position and aligns the airplane on the runway center/takeoff path.
- Lift off at the recommended airspeed and accelerates to V_Y.
- Establish a pitch attitude that will maintain V_Y +10/-5 knots.
- Retract the landing gear, if appropriate, and flaps after a positive rate of climb is established.
- Maintain takeoff power to a safe maneuvering altitude.
- Maintain directional control and proper wind-drift correction throughout the takeoff and climb.
- Comply with noise abatement procedures.
- Complete the appropriate checklist.

11 — Crosswind Takeoff And Climb

A crosswind takeoff is much like a normal takeoff, except you have to use the flight controls to counteract the crosswind component. The term crosswind component refers to that part of the wind which acts at a right angle to the airplane's path on takeoff or landing. You can calculate this component with a crosswind component chart or with a flight computer.

You should always use the aircraft manufacturer's recommended takeoff checklist. Takeoffs with strong crosswinds are normally made with the minimum flap setting necessary for the field length. This helps reduce the drift angle immediately after takeoff. The POH normally lists a maximum demonstrated crosswind component for takeoff and landing. Your personal crosswind limit is based on your skill level, as well as any limitation specified by your instructor during training. In addition, flight training operators often have specified limits based on pilot experience and/or proficiency.

 Complete the before takeoff check. With the exception of the oil temperature gauge, all engine instruments must register within the normal operating range prior to takeoff.

 Ensure that the runway, as well as the approach and departure paths are clear of other aircraft.

 After obtaining a clearance (at a controlled airport) or self announcing your intentions (at an uncontrolled airport), taxi onto the runway and line up with the runway centerline. Center the nosewheel and check the windsock to determine the wind position in relation to the runway.

- Fully turn the yoke in the direction of the wind, placing the upwind aileron in the up position. For example, if the crosswind is blowing from your left, fully turn the yoke to the left, placing the left aileron in the up position. This control deflection compensates for the crosswind's tendency to push and roll the airplane to the downwind side of the runway.

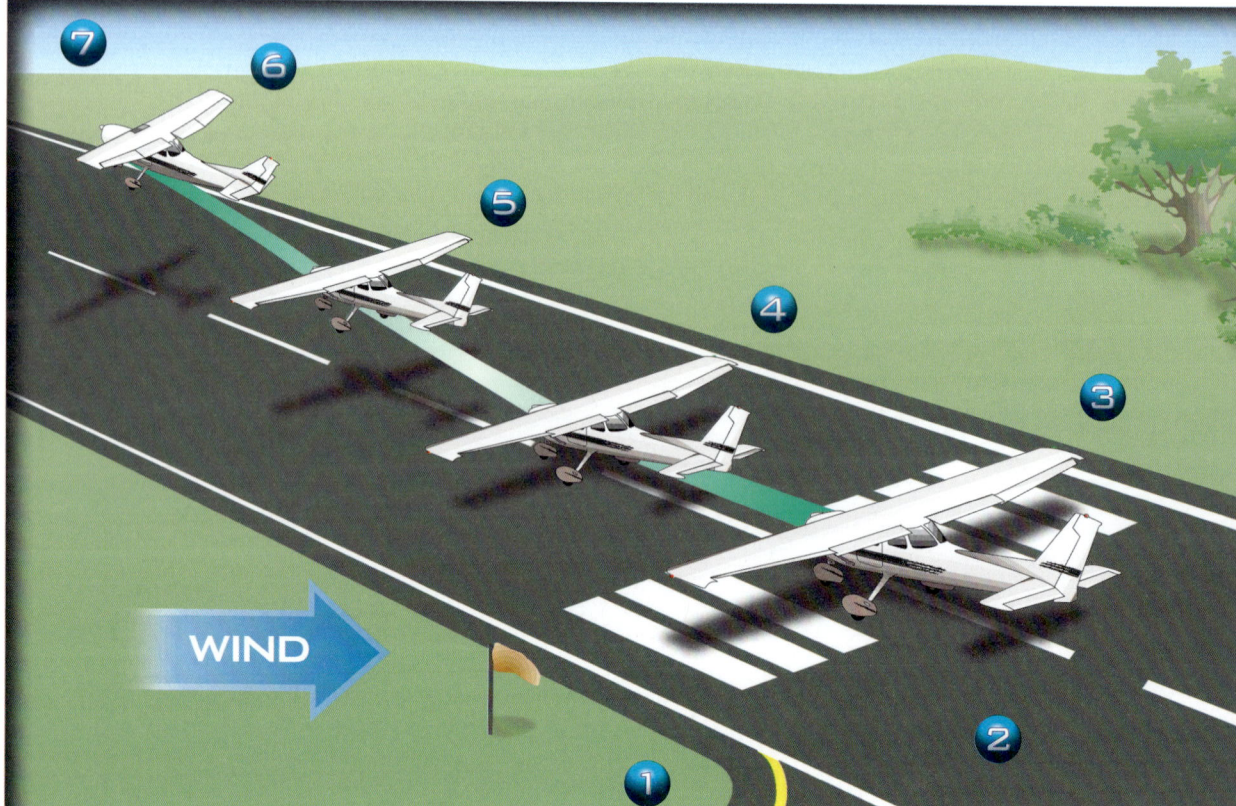

CROSSWIND TAKEOFF AND CLIMB

- Advance the throttle smoothly to takeoff power, and as the airplane starts to roll, select a point on the cowl through which the centerline of the runway passes and use it as a reference point for directional control.

- Check the engine instruments to ensure the engine is developing full power and is functioning within its operational limits. Slow acceleration or any hesitation in power is sufficient reason to discontinue the takeoff.

- Counteract the airplane's weathervaning tendency with rudder application.

 As the airplane accelerates and the controls become more effective, reduce the aileron deflection gradually so it is just sufficient to counteract the rolling tendency. Apply right rudder pressure as necessary to compensate for engine torque.

The amount of aileron and rudder deflection required to compensate for a crosswind depends on the crosswind component. When you use the right amount of crosswind correction, the airplane tracks straight down the runway and you feel no side load on the landing gear.

To allow the airplane to have a greater airspeed on liftoff with increased control capabilities, hold the airplane on the runway until you attain a slightly higher-than-normal liftoff speed. Then, lift the airplane off the runway promptly and establish a normal climb attitude. This technique also reduces the chance of the airplane being lifted off prematurely by a sudden gust of wind.

Accelerate to the initial climb speed recommended by the manufacturer and adjust the pitch attitude to maintain that airspeed. To track straight out on an imaginary extension of the runway centerline, enter a crab by making a coordinated turn into the wind.

Once you have reached a safe altitude, adjust the power to the recommended climb setting and trim the aircraft to relieve any control pressures. Complete the appropriate checklist procedures and depart or remain in the traffic pattern.

If a control tower is in operation, you can request and usually receive approval for a nonstandard departure. The standard procedure for departing an uncontrolled airport is to fly straight-out or to make a 45° turn in the direction of the traffic pattern.

 CROSSWIND TAKEOFF AND CLIMB

To meet the PTS requirements, you must:

- Exhibit knowledge of the elements related to a normal and crosswind takeoff, climb operations, and rejected takeoff procedures.
- Position the flight controls for the existing wind conditions.
- Clear the area; taxi into the takeoff position and align the airplane on the runway center/takeoff path.
- Lift off at the recommended airspeed and accelerates to V_Y.
- Establish a pitch attitude that will maintain V_Y +10/-5 knots.
- Retract the landing gear, if appropriate, and flaps after a positive rate of climb is established.
- Maintain takeoff power to a safe maneuvering altitude.
- Maintain directional control and proper wind-drift correction throughout the takeoff and climb.
- Comply with noise abatement procedures.
- Complete the appropriate checklist.

12 — TRAFFIC PATTERNS

Standard traffic patterns are used to improve both the safety and efficiency of airport operations. They are particularly important at airports without operating control towers. The standard traffic pattern is rectangular and has five named legs; downwind, base, final, departure, and crosswind. The direction of the pattern refers to the orientation of the pattern turns. For example, aircraft in a left-hand traffic pattern make left turns to base, final, crosswind, and downwind. Normally, a left-hand pattern is used to give the left-seat pilot the best view of the runway and the surrounding environment. In some cases, a right-hand traffic pattern may be used to avoid obstacles, terrain, restricted airspace, noise sensitive areas, or other runways. Both left-hand and right-hand traffic patterns normally are used when simultaneous operations are conducted on parallel runways. Other special considerations may require additional variations to the standard traffic pattern. You can find information regarding specific airport traffic patterns in the *Airport/Facility Directory, Aeronautical Information Manual, FAR Part 93,* and Notices to Airmen (NOTAMs).

Collision avoidance rests with you, the pilot in command. Airport operations require a constant effort to see and avoid other aircraft. You should make a point of checking both the approach and departure ends of the runway prior to takeoff or landing.

Listed below are a few collision avoidance procedures you can use at both controlled and uncontrolled airports.
- Use anticollision and landing lights in the traffic pattern and within a 10-mile radius of the airport.
- During climb out, accelerate to cruise climb airspeed as soon as practical.
- Prior to all turns, check for traffic.
- Monitor the appropriate radio frequency and listen for information concerning other air traffic.

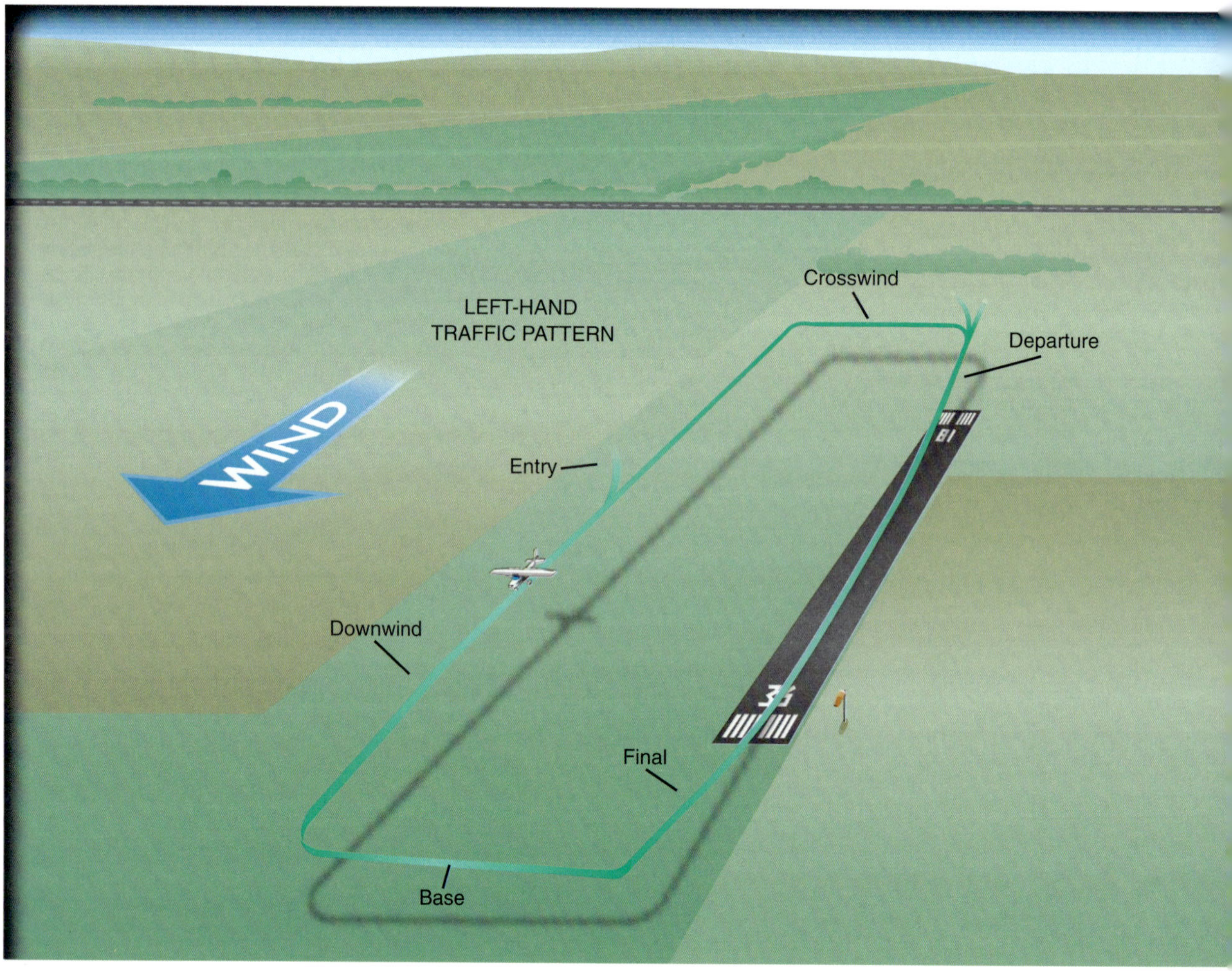

TRAFFIC PATTERNS

A runway incursion is an occurrence at an airport involving an aircraft, vehicle, person, or object on the ground that creates a collision hazard or results in loss of proper separation with an aircraft taking off or landing. Runway incursions usually are caused by errors associated with clearances, communications, airport surface movement, and positional awareness.

Listed below are a few recommended procedures that are beneficial in avoiding runway incursions.

- Review the Notices to Airmen (NOTAMs) regarding airport construction and lighting.
- While taxiing, monitor the appropriate radio frequency and concentrate on your primary responsibilities. Do not become absorbed in other tasks or conversation while the aircraft is moving.
- At a controlled airport, if unsure of your position, request progressive taxi instructions.
- During periods of reduced visibility, or at night, make sure others can see you. Use your exterior landing/taxi lights, when practical and position lights, when required.
- To help maintain situational awareness, take time to familiarize yourself with the airport layout by studying the airport diagram.

In addition to collision avoidance precautions, anytime you operate in close proximity to other aircraft, such as in the traffic pattern, you should be aware of the increased potential for wake turbulence encounters. When possible, avoiding the area below and behind other aircraft should prevent you from experiencing most of the in-flight hazards associated with wake turbulence.

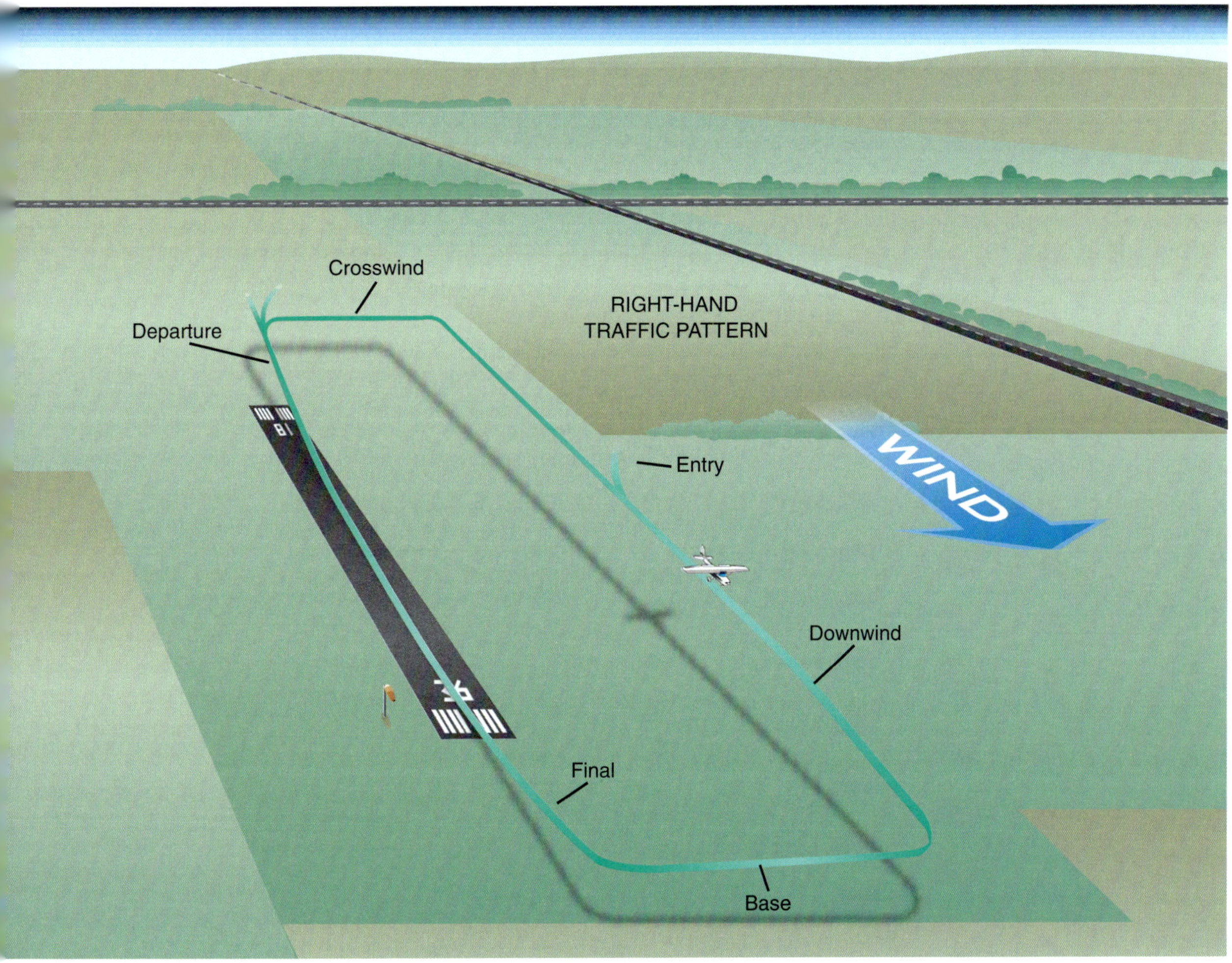

TRAFFIC PATTERNS

Since wind shear can occur during traffic pattern operations, you also should be knowledgeable of the conditions favorable for wind shear. Anticipate wind shear when frontal systems and thunderstorms are in the area.

At airports with operating control towers (controlled airports), you are required by regulations to establish and maintain radio communication with the tower. At airports without control towers (uncontrolled airports), you are not required to have or use a radio. However, if your aircraft is radio equipped while operating within 10 miles of any airport, you should monitor and communicate on the common traffic advisory frequency (CTAF). The CTAF may be a UNICOM, MULTICOM, flight service station (FSS), or tower frequency. Before you transmit on the CTAF, you should monitor the frequency for a short period of time to get a picture of the traffic situation and determine a plan of action for entry to the pattern. When making your radio calls, always report your aircraft identification, position, and intentions. Also be sure to include the name of the airport in broadcasts, since more than one airport may be assigned the same frequency. An example of a radio call requesting airport information is as follows: *"Coronado UNICOM, Cessna 23455, 10 miles northwest descending through 4,000, landing Coronado, request wind and runway information Coronado."*

In the absence of an FSS, UNICOM operator, or operating control tower, you should overfly the airport at least 500 feet above the traffic pattern altitude to determine the landing runway and the associated pattern direction. Use visual indicators such as the segmented circle, wind direction indicator, landing direction indicator, or traffic pattern indicator. An example of a radio call for an aircraft conducting an overflight of the airport to determine the landing information is as follows: *"Coronado traffic, Cessna 23455, 10 miles south descending through 4,000, overflying for landing Coronado."*

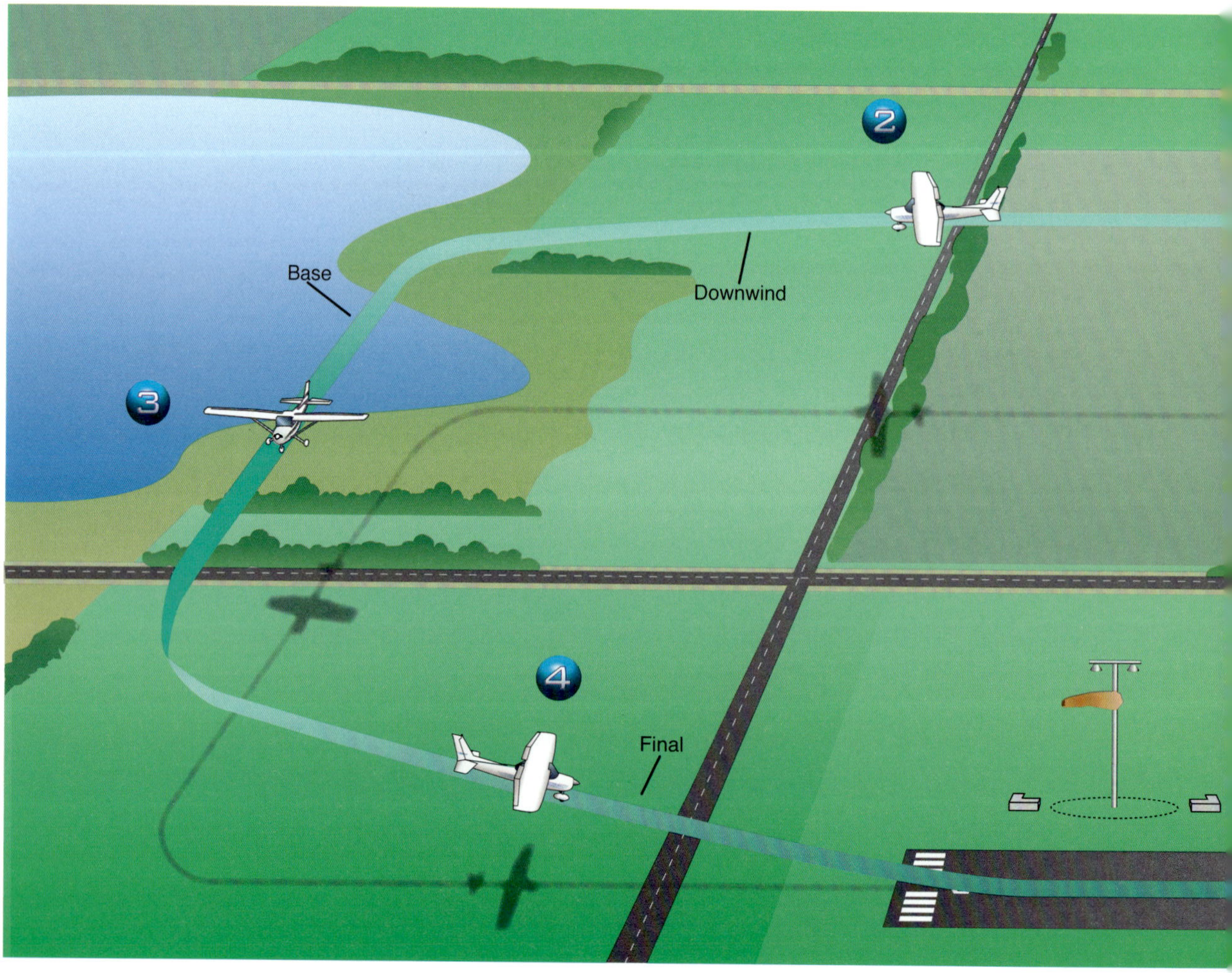

TRAFFIC PATTERNS

 Enter the traffic pattern at a 45° angle to the downwind leg, abeam the midpoint of the runway, at pattern altitude (normally 1,000 feet AGL). An example of a radio call at an uncontrolled airport is as follows: *"Coronado traffic, Cessna 23455, entering downwind for Runway 9, touch-and-go, Coronado."*

It is good practice to establish your aircraft at pattern altitude while well clear of the pattern prior to entry.

 Fly the **downwind leg** parallel to the runway. Maintain pattern altitude until at the 180° position, or position abeam the intended landing point. At the 180° position, begin your descent for landing.

You may have to delay the start of your descent to follow other traffic in the pattern.

 Turn onto the **base leg** when the touchdown point is approximately 45° behind the inside wingtip. An example of a radio call at an uncontrolled airport is as follows: *"Coronado traffic Cessna 23455, base, Runway 9, touch-and-go, Coronado."*

The turn to base should be accomplished using approximately 30° angle of bank. Adjust the base leg to follow other traffic and compensate for the prevailing wind conditions. For example, with a strong wind you will need to begin your turn to base leg sooner than normal so that you do not drift too far downwind during your turn.

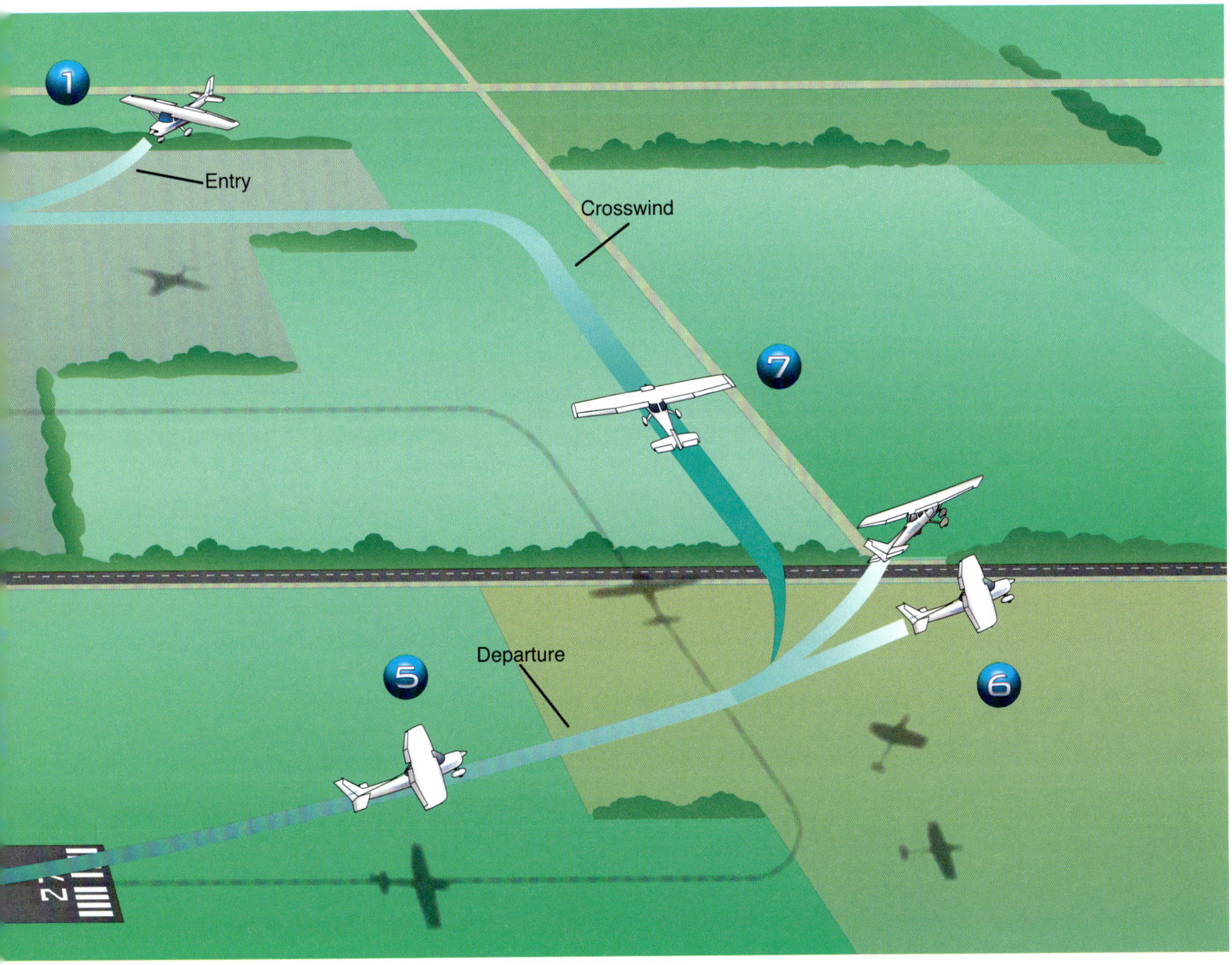

Traffic Patterns

4. Complete the turn to **final approach** at least one-quarter of a mile from the approach end of the runway. Fly along an imaginary extension of the runway centerline, compensating for crosswind conditions as needed. An example of a radio call at an uncontrolled airport is as follows: *"Coronado traffic, Cessna 23455, final, Runway 9, touch and go, Coronado."*

Your turn to final should be accomplished by using between 20° and 30° angle of bank. The turn should be completed at a safe altitude above the terrain, obstructions, and the airport elevation. When approaching a set of parallel runways, it is extremely important to avoid overshooting the final approach and interfering with the parallel runway traffic.

5. On the **departure leg,** climb out on runway heading until you are beyond the departure end of the runway and within 300 feet of pattern altitude. An example of a radio call at an uncontrolled airport for an aircraft remaining in the pattern is as follows: *"Coronado traffic, Cessna 23455, departing Runway 9, remaining in the pattern, Coronado."*

Be sure to maintain a track over the ground that corresponds to the runway extended centerline. If you are familiar with the airport, you may want to use ground checkpoints to maintain your track; a crosswind can cause you to drift off the extended centerline even though you maintain runway heading. If traffic causes you to extend your departure, be sure to level off at pattern altitude.

6. If you are departing the traffic pattern, continue your climb to pattern altitude, then fly straight out, or exit with a 45° turn to the pattern side of the runway. In either case, you should comply with the departure procedures established for that airport. An example of a radio call at an uncontrolled airport for an aircraft departing the traffic pattern is as follows: *"Coronado traffic, Cessna 23455, departing Runway 9, departing the traffic pattern to the northeast, climbing to 5,500, Coronado."*

If you are operating from one of a set of parallel runways, be sure your ground track does not penetrate the departure path of the other runway(s). Unless regulations or local procedures dictate otherwise, you should monitor/communicate on the CTAF until 10 miles from the airport.

7. If you are staying in the traffic pattern, continue your climb to pattern altitude on the **crosswind leg**. Once at pattern altitude, level off and continue to fly 90° to the runway until you are ready to turn downwind.

Be sure to check for other traffic in the pattern before starting your turn to crosswind. If necessary, extend your departure leg to follow other aircraft.

TRAFFIC PATTERNS

To meet the PTS requirements, you must:

- Exhibit knowledge of the elements related to traffic patterns. This shall include procedures at airports with and without operating control towers, prevention of runway incursions, collision avoidance, wake turbulence avoidance, and wind shear.

- Comply with proper traffic pattern procedures.

- Maintain proper spacing from other aircraft.

- Correct for wind drift to maintain the proper ground track.

- Maintain orientation with the runway/landing area in use.

- Maintain traffic pattern altitude, ±100 feet (30 meters), and the appropriate airspeed, ±10 knots.

13 — NORMAL APPROACH AND LANDING

The successful landing of an aircraft is probably the most challenging, as well as satisfying, phase of a flight. Every landing is different due to varying wind conditions, runway surface and length, and possible obstructions at the approach end of the runway. In addition, the airplane can be configured for landing with no flaps, partial flaps, or full flaps. When you use full flaps for landing, you will typically extend the first increment of flaps on the downwind leg and the next on base leg. Usually, you will extend full flaps on the final approach leg. Since the full-flap stall speed is less than the no-flap or partial-flap stall speed, landing with full flaps results in a slower touchdown speed and shorter ground roll. The following discussion provides general procedures for a no-flap landing in a tricycle gear airplane.

APPROACH

Prior to each landing, you should complete a before landing check using a printed checklist as recommended by the aircraft manufacturer. As you fly the traffic pattern and approach to landing, be sure to self-announce your position and/or intentions on the appropriate frequency in accordance with recommended procedures or communicate with the control tower, as appropriate.

1 On downwind, ensure that the before landing checklist is completed and clear the area ahead and to the left and right of your flight path for other traffic. In addition, check for traffic which may be above and descending or below and climbing through your flight path.

- As you approach the 180° position, or position abeam the intended landing point, you should be at the designated traffic pattern altitude near the airplane's cruising speed.

- At the 180° position, establish the descent power setting while maintaining altitude to allow the airplane to slow to approach speed.

- Maintain the approach speed recommended by the manufacturer and initiate a descent.

NORMAL APPROACH AND LANDING

You may need to delay the descent if the downwind leg must be extended to follow traffic. Avoid becoming so engrossed with in-cockpit duties that you are unable to maintain situational awareness.

2. Check for traffic on the base leg and on the extended runway centerline of the final approach. Begin your turn to the base leg after the airplane has descended 100 to 200 feet and the landing point is approximately 45° behind the wing.

As you turn to base, the wind tends to push the airplane away from the runway. Therefore, it usually is necessary to turn more than 90° to apply the appropriate crab angle.

3. As the airplane rolls out on base, you are at the key position, an early decision point where you must assess your situation. At the key position you should make any adjustments to altitude, airspeed, and distance from the runway to ensure a smooth approach and to avoid large or abrupt last minute corrections on short final.

If the airplane is high at the key position, you should either reduce power, extend additional flaps, or both to avoid landing beyond your desired touchdown point. If the airplane is low or wide on base leg, or if the wind is stronger than normal, you could land short of your desired point. Therefore, you should either begin your turn to final sooner, or add power. Retracting flaps is not considered an acceptable correction.

4. Check the final approach path for traffic and, if clear, start your turn.

- Roll out on final approach between 300 and 500 feet above ground level, and approximately one-quarter mile from the end of the runway.

If you are flying an airplane with retractable landing gear, re-check that the landing gear is down and locked.

- Maintain the recommended approach speed. If an approach speed is not recommended in the POH, use a final approach speed that is 1.3 times the power-off stall speed in the landing configuration ($1.3V_{S0}$).
- Use outside visual references to determine the proper descent angle, or glide path.

If you maintain a constant descent angle, the apparent shape of the runway will remain unchanged. If your approach becomes shallower, the runway will appear to shorten and become wider. Conversely, if your approach is steepened, the runway will appear to be longer and narrower. If you maintain a constant descent angle, the sides of the runway will maintain the same relationship and the threshold will remain in a fixed position in relation to the airplane's nose.

NORMAL APPROACH AND LANDING

- Simultaneously adjust pitch and power as necessary to control descent angle and airspeed. If a deviation in pitch attitude, power, airspeed, or wind condition occurs, make an appropriate control change to maintain the proper descent angle.

> The following techniques are recommended to correct for deviations from the correct descent angle and airspeed on final approach.
>
> - Descent angle is too steep (airplane is too high) and airspeed is too high; reduce power and gradually increase the pitch attitude.
> - Descent angle is too steep and airspeed is correct; reduce power and maintain pitch attitude.
> - Descent angle is too steep and airspeed is too low; reduce power and decrease the pitch attitude.
> - Descent angle is too shallow (airplane is too low) and airspeed is correct; add power and maintain the pitch attitude.
> - Descent angle is too shallow and airspeed is too low; add power and decrease the pitch attitude slightly. You should increase the power anytime the airplane is low and slow. Do not try to stretch a glide by applying back pressure on the yoke to increase pitch attitude without adding power.
>
> As you approach the proper descent angle and airspeed after making a correction, readjust the power and pitch to maintain the correct attitude and trim to relieve control pressures.

- Estimate the point at which the airplane will actually touch down by finding the point where the descent angle intersects the ground and adding the approximate distance to be traveled in the flare. The descent angle intersection point, also called the aiming point, is the spot on the ground that has no apparent relative movement. As the airplane descends, all objects beyond the aiming point appear to move away from the airplane, while objects closer appear to move toward it.

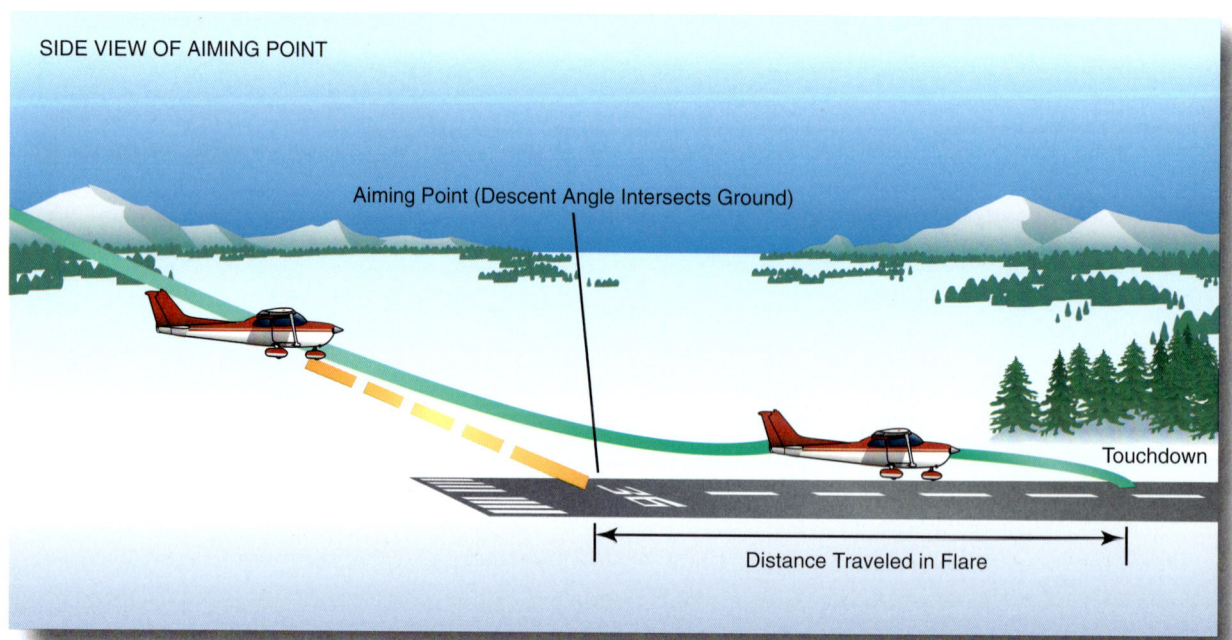

LANDING

During the landing you use a combination of visual and kinesthetic cues. Practicing descents, slow flight, and power-off stalls helps to increase your sensitivity to control responses and allows you to develop smooth control application. However, your kinesthetic sense may not be fully developed at the time you begin landing practice and you must rely primarily on visual cues. The landing consists of three elements — the flare, the touchdown, and the roll-out. The term **flare** refers to the process of changing the attitude of the airplane from a glide or descent to a landing attitude. Its purpose is to reduce speed and decrease the rate of descent. The flare begins at different altitudes for airplanes at varying weights and approach speeds. However, for most training airplanes it begins at approximately 10 to 20 feet above the ground.

SIDE VIEW OF FLARE

 FLARE

- Begin the flare approximately 10 to 20 feet above the runway by gradually increasing back pressure on the yoke to reduce speed and decrease the rate of descent.

- Focus at an intermediate point between the nose of the airplane and a distance down the runway. During the flare, you must look to one side of the airplane, since its nose may block your view ahead.

- The airplane should reach a near-zero rate of descent approximately 1 foot above the runway at about 8 to 10 knots above a stall speed with the power at idle.

- Attempt to hold the airplane just off the runway by increasing back pressure. This causes the airplane to settle slowly to the runway in a slightly nose-high attitude as it approaches stall speed.

Use a visual comparison of the size of known objects on the ground, or depth perception, to determine the attitude for the flare and the height throughout the flare. The area where you focus your vision during the approach is important. For example, if you focus too close to the airplane, the airspeed blurs objects on the ground and your actions may be too abrupt. If you focus too far down the runway, you may be unable to accurately judge height above the ground and your reactions will be slow. In this situation, you may allow the airplane to fly onto the runway without flaring.

 TOUCHDOWN

- Touch down on the main landing gear in a nose-high attitude with the engine idling and the airplane at minimum controllable airspeed.

NORMAL APPROACH AND LANDING

> As the airplane touches down, your heels should be on the floor so there is no tendency to use the brakes inadvertently.

- Use the rudder to keep the airplane's longitudinal axis parallel to the direction the airplane is moving along the runway.

- Hold back pressure on the yoke to maintain a positive angle of attack for aerodynamic braking and to hold the nosewheel off the ground.

- As the airplane decelerates, gradually relax back pressure to allow the nosewheel to gently settle onto the runway.

> Flying the airplane onto the runway with excess speed can cause floating or skipping and may result in a loss of directional control.

7 ROLL-OUT

- Maintain directional control with the rudder to keep the airplane on the centerline of the runway.

- Clear the runway and complete the after landing checklist. Taxi to the designated parking or refueling area.

NORMAL APPROACH AND LANDING

To meet the PTS requirements, you must:

- Exhibit knowledge of the elements related to a normal and crosswind approach and landing.

- Consider the wind conditions, landing surface, obstructions, and select a suitable touchdown point.

- Establish the recommended approach and landing configuration and airspeed, and adjust pitch attitude and power as required.

- Maintain a stabilized approach and recommended airspeed, or in its absence, not more than 1.3 V_{S0}, +10/-5 knots, with wind gust factor applied.

- Make smooth, timely, and correct control application during the roundout and touchdown.

- Touch down smoothly at approximate stalling speed.

- Touch down at or within 400 feet (120 meters) beyond a specified point, with no drift, and with the airplane's longitudinal axis aligned with and over the runway center/landing path.

- Maintain crosswind correction and directional control throughout the approach and landing sequence.

- Complete the appropriate checklist.

FORWARD SLIP TO A LANDING

A forward slip may be used to steepen the airplane's descent angle to dissipate altitude without increasing airspeed. This is accomplished by exposing as much of the airplane's surface to the oncoming air as possible, so the airplane's frontal area produces considerable drag. A forward slip can be valuable when you are landing in fields with obstructions. In an airplane with side-by-side

Normal Approach And Landing

seating, you will usually slip to the left since this provides you with an excellent view of the landing area during the entire slip.

You should perform forward slips with the engine at idle power to increase the rate of descent. To initiate a forward slip, lower one wing by turning the yoke and at the same time, apply opposite rudder to keep the airplane from turning in the direction of the lowered wing. The airplane's nose will angle away from the runway, however the airplane's ground track remains in alignment with the extended centerline of the runway. To prevent the airspeed from increasing, raise the nose slightly above the normal gliding position. As soon as you lose sufficient altitude, begin the recovery by raising the low wing and simultaneously easing rudder pressure. Level the wings and adjust the pitch attitude to a normal glide.

Another type of slip is the sideslip which is used to compensate for drift during crosswind landings. During a sideslip, the airplane's longitudinal axis remains parallel to the original flight path and is aligned with the runway. You will learn more about performing sideslips when you examine crosswind landings.

FORWARD SLIP TO A LANDING

To meet the PTS requirements, you must:

- Exhibit knowledge of the elements related to a normal and crosswind approach and landing.

- Consider the wind conditions, landing surface, obstructions, and select a suitable touchdown point.

- Establish the slipping attitude at the point from which a landing can be made using the recommended approach and landing configuration and airspeed; adjusts pitch attitude and power as required.

- Maintain a ground track aligned with the runway center/landing path and an airspeed, which results in minimum float during the roundout.

- Make smooth, timely, and correct control application during the recovery from the slip, the roundout and the touchdown.

- Touch down smoothly at approximate stalling speed, at or within 400 feet (120 meters) beyond a specified point, with no side drift, and with the airplane's longitudinal axis aligned with and over the runway center/landing path.

- Maintain crosswind correction and directional control throughout the approach and landing sequence.

- Complete the appropriate checklist.

Go-Around

Generally, if the airplane has not touched down in the first third of the runway, you should execute a go-around, and set up for another landing. The go-around also may be necessary when obstacles are on the runway or when you feel uncomfortable with the approach due to incorrect procedures or other unsafe conditions. At times, you may perform landings that cause the airplane to bounce into the air. Usually, it is wise not to attempt to salvage these landings and you should make an immediate go-around. The decision to make a go-around should be positive, and you should make it before a critical situation develops. Once the decision has been made, it should be implemented without hesitation.

Normal Approach and Landing

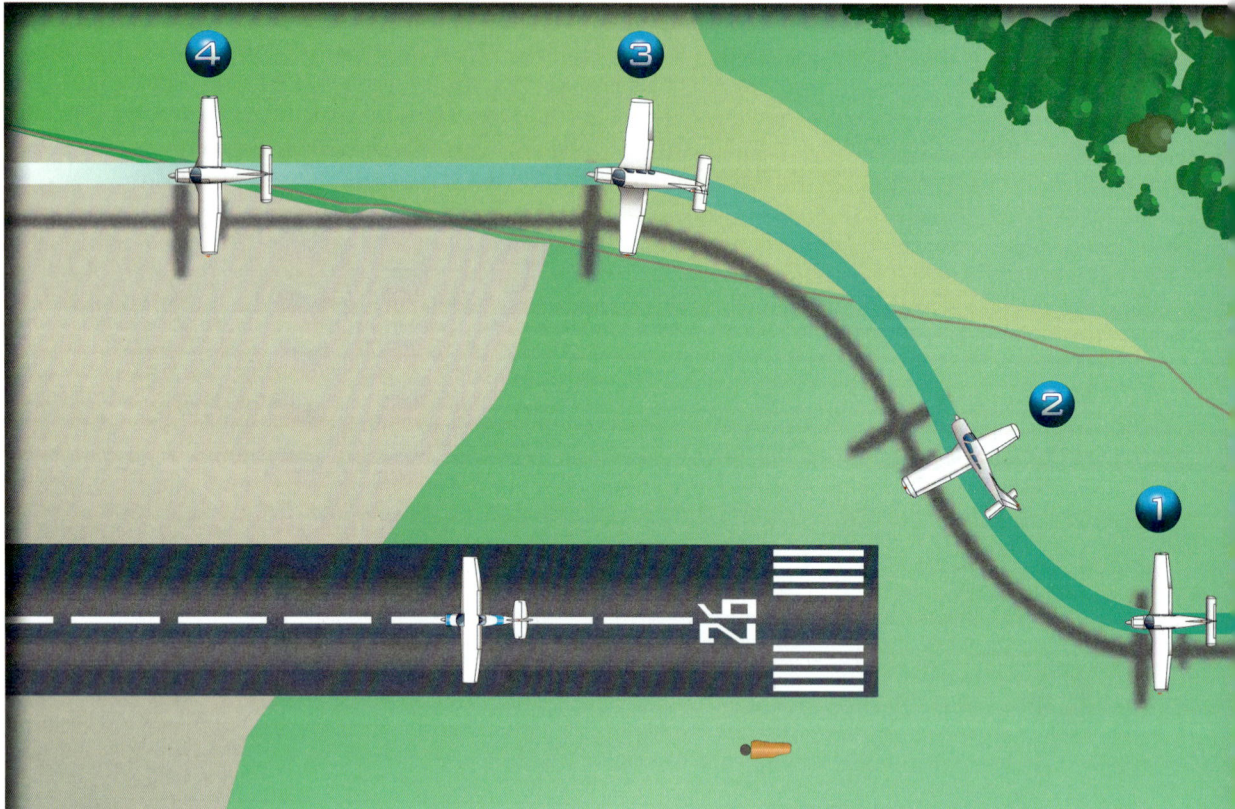

 Apply takeoff power *immediately*, place the carburetor heat in the OFF position, and adjust the airplane's pitch attitude to slow or stop the descent. After the descent has been stopped, partially retract the flaps (if applicable) as recommended by the manufacturer.

When full power is applied, it is usually necessary to hold a considerable amount of forward pressure on the yoke since the airplane was trimmed for approach. In addition, right rudder pressure must be applied to counteract torque and P-factor. To help keep the airplane in a safe climbing attitude, trim the airplane to relieve the heavy control pressures.

Caution must be used when retracting the flaps. Typically it is recommended that the flaps be retracted in small increments to allow the airplane to accelerate as they are raised. A premature retraction of flaps causes a loss of lift which could result in the airplane settling back to the runway.

 Establish a positive rate of climb. If another aircraft is on the runway, make a shallow turn to the non-pattern side of the runway, then turn parallel to the runway. In this position, you can see the runway and other aircraft clearly.

Special cases, such as the use of parallel runways, may prevent you from making a turn.

 Retract the landing gear (if applicable), and accelerate to V_Y before retracting the remaining flaps. Trim to relieve control pressures.

Since full flaps produce more drag than extended landing gear, it is generally recommended that the flaps be at least partially retracted before retracting the gear. This also prevents damage if the airplane inadvertently touches down on the runway as the go-around is initiated.

NORMAL APPROACH AND LANDING

 After you have the airplane under control and have reached a safe altitude, self-announce your position and/or intentions on the appropriate frequency in accordance with recommended procedures or communicate with the control tower, as appropriate. Maintain directional control and apply proper wind drift as you continue the flight parallel to the departure leg. When you reach the crosswind leg allow for proper spacing, check for traffic, and then reenter the traffic pattern as appropriate.

GO-AROUND

To meet the PTS requirements, you must:

- Exhibit knowledge of the elements related to a go-around/rejected landing.

- Make a timely decision to discontinue the approach to landing.

- Apply takeoff power immediately and transition to climb pitch attitude for V_Y, and maintain V_Y +10/-5 knots.

- Retract the flaps as appropriate.

- Retract the landing gear, if appropriate, after a positive rate of climb is established.

- Maneuver to the side of the runway/landing area to clear and avoid conflicting traffic.

- Maintain takeoff power to a safe maneuvering altitude.

- Maintain directional control and proper wind-drift correction throughout the climb.

- Complete the appropriate checklist.

14 — CROSSWIND APPROACH AND LANDING

There are two basic techniques used to accomplish a crosswind approach and landing — the crab method and the wing-low, or sideslip, method. The crab method requires you to establish a heading (crab) into the wind on final approach with the wings level so that the airplane's ground track remains aligned with the extended centerline of the runway. The crab angle is maintained until just prior to touchdown, when the longitudinal axis of the airplane must be quickly aligned with the runway to avoid imposing any side loads on the main landing gear.

Since the crab method requires a high degree of judgment and timing, the wing-low method is normally preferred for executing crosswind landings. The wing-low method of crosswind approach and landing is described here. Since the same general procedures used to execute a normal approach and landing apply to a crosswind approach and landing, only the additional techniques required for wind correction are explained in this discussion. The wing-low method enables you to simultaneously keep the airplane's ground track and the longitudinal axis aligned with the runway centerline throughout the final approach, flare, touchdown, and roll-out. This technique prevents the airplane from touching down sideways, imposing damaging side loads on the landing gear.

The degree to which flaps should be extended in a crosswind varies with the airplane's handling characteristics, as well as the wind velocity. Full flaps may be used if the crosswind component is not in excess of the airplane's capability or unless the manufacturer recommends otherwise.

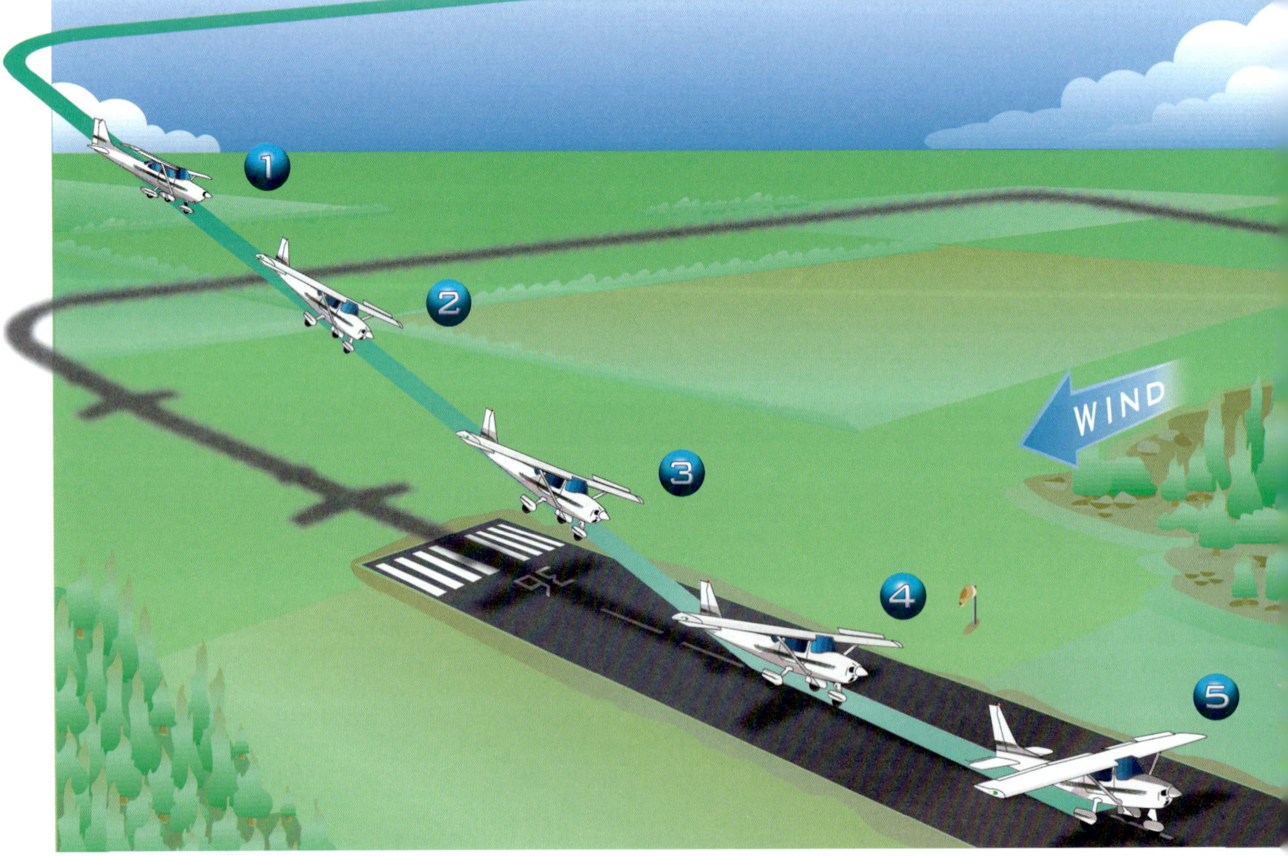

APPROACH

If the crosswind exists at traffic pattern altitude as well as near the surface, you must apply the proper wind correction (crab) in the traffic pattern so your ground track remains rectangular. Since the wind direction is perpendicular to the runway, you must crab into the wind on the downwind leg to remain parallel to the runway. On base leg, you will either encounter a tailwind or headwind. Your groundspeed increases with a tailwind component and you may need to start your turn to final sooner than normal and/or use up to 30° of bank to avoid overshooting the runway. When encountering a headwind on base leg, avoid turning too early or using too much bank angle so you do not undershoot the runway.

CROSSWIND APPROACH AND LANDING

 Complete the turn to final on an extension of the runway centerline with the airplane in a crab to correct for wind drift.

 Align the airplane's heading with the runway centerline, note the rate and direction of drift, and then apply correction by lowering the upwind wing. Simultaneously apply opposite rudder to prevent the airplane from turning and keep the longitudinal axis aligned with the runway. For example, if the crosswind is blowing from your left, turn the yoke to the left, placing the left aileron in the up position and apply right rudder.

If the crosswind diminishes, your wind correction must be reduced or the airplane will no longer be aligned with the runway centerline. If the crosswind is very strong, you may not have sufficient rudder travel available to compensate for the strong turning tendency caused by the lowered wing. In this situation, you must go-around and land on a runway with more favorable wind conditions.

LANDING

Maintaining accurate directional control while the airplane's speed is decreasing is a challenge during crosswind landings.

 ## FLARE

- As airspeed decreases in the flare, the flight controls become less effective and you must gradually increase the rudder and aileron deflection to maintain the proper amount of wind correction.

 ## TOUCHDOWN

- Maintain the crosswind correction as the airplane touches down. Initially, the airplane will touch down on the upwind wheel and then as forward momentum decreases, the weight of the airplane causes the downwind main wheel to gradually settle onto the runway.

- Since you are holding opposite rudder pressure to correct for the crosswind, the nosewheel may not be aligned with the runway as the airplane touches down. To prevent swerving on the runway, you must relax the corrective rudder pressure just as the nosewheel touches down.

 ## ROLL-OUT

- Maintain directional control with the rudder while keeping the upwind wing from rising by use of the aileron.

- As the airplane decelerates and the controls become less effective, increase your wind correction with the ailerons. Turn the yoke fully into the wind as the airplane slows to a taxi speed. Clear the runway and complete the after landing checklist.

CROSSWIND APPROACH AND LANDING

To meet the PTS requirements, you must:

- Exhibit knowledge of the elements related to a normal and crosswind approach and landing.
- Adequately survey the intended landing area.
- Consider the wind conditions, landing surface, obstructions, and select a suitable touchdown point.
- Establish the recommended approach and landing configuration and airspeed, and adjust pitch attitude and power as required.
- Maintain a stabilized approach and recommended airspeed, or in it absence, not more than 1.3 V_{SO}, +10/-5 knots, with wind gust factor applied.
- Make smooth, timely, and correct control application during the roundout and touchdown.
- Touch down smoothly at approximate stalling speed.
- Touch down at or within 400 feet (120 meters) beyond a specified point, with no drift, and with the airplane's longitudinal axis aligned with and over the runway center/landing path.
- Maintain crosswind correction and directional control throughout the approach and landing sequence.
- Complete the appropriate checklist.

EXERCISES — AIRPORT OPERATIONS

10 — Normal Takeoff and Climb

1. What action should you take if the engine is not developing sufficient power for takeoff?

2. How can you counteract the left-turning tendency caused by engine torque on takeoff?

3. Why should you keep your hand on the throttle throughout the takeoff?

4. What can occur if you attempt to lift off with an excessively nose-high attitude?

5. After a normal takeoff at an uncontrolled airport, what are the recommended procedures for leaving the local area?

11 — Crosswind Takeoff and Climb

1. How can you determine the maximum demonstrated crosswind component for your airplane?

2. True/False. To counteract the effects of a crosswind from the left during takeoff, you should turn the yoke to the right, placing the left aileron in the down position. _____

3. As the airplane accelerates during the takeoff roll, will you normally need to increase or decrease aileron deflection used to compensate for a crosswind? _____

4. How can you determine if you are using the proper amount of crosswind correction?

5. After takeoff, what action can you take to track straight out on an imaginary extension of the runway centerline?

Exercises — Airport Operations

12 — Traffic Patterns

1. What are the five named legs of the traffic pattern?

2. True/False. Both left-hand and right-hand traffic patterns are normally used when simultaneous operations are conducted on parallel runways. _____

3. To aid in collision avoidance, you should turn on your airplane's landing light within how many miles of the airport? _____

4. In the absence of an FSS, UNICOM operator, or operating control tower, you should overfly the airport at least how many feet above the traffic pattern altitude? _____

5. Your airplane is Piper 9163K and you are practicing touch-and-go landings to Runway 26 at Front Range Airport (uncontrolled). Provide an example of the proper radio call after completing the turn to final.

13 — Normal Approach and Landing

1. True/False. Landing with full flaps extended results in a faster touchdown speed and ground roll. _____

2. At what position on the downwind should you normally begin your descent for landing?

3. What corrective actions can you take if the airplane is high when you reach the key position?

4. While on final approach, if the airplane's descent angle is too shallow and the airspeed is too low, what action should you take?

5. The landing phase of flight can be divided into what three elements?

6. While maintaining directional control with the rudder pedals, why should your heels be on the floor as the airplane touches down?

7. During landing, floating can be caused by what error?

8. What is the primary purpose of the forward slip?

9. True/False. While executing a forward slip, the airplane's longitudinal axis is aligned with the runway. _____

10. What is the first step you should take when initiating a go-around?

14 — Crosswind Approach and Landing

1. What are the two basic methods used for crosswind landings?

2. If you experience a tailwind on base leg, what action(s) can you take to avoid overshooting the runway when turning onto final approach?

3. If you encounter a crosswind from the right on final approach and landing, how should you position the controls to compensate for wind drift?
    A.   Turn the yoke to the left and apply left rudder pressure.
    B.   Turn the yoke to the left and apply right rudder pressure.
    C.   Turn the yoke to the right and apply left rudder pressure.

4. While making a crosswind correction on final approach, what action should you take if you do not have sufficient rudder travel available?

5. As the airplane decelerates during the roll-out, will you need to increase or decrease aileron deflection to counteract a steady crosswind?

EMERGENCY LANDING PROCEDURES

EMERGENCY LANDING PROCEDURES

EMERGENCY LANDING PROCEDURES

MANEUVER 15 4-2
SYSTEMS AND EQUIPMENT
MALFUNCTIONS

MANEUVER 16 4-4
EMERGENCY DESCENT

MANEUVER 17 4-6
EMERGENCY APPROACH AND LANDING

EXERCISES 4-11

Video Volume I — Ground Operations, Basic Maneuvers, Airport Operations, and Emergency Landing Procedures

Computer Training — Emergency Landing Procedures

SYSTEMS AND EQUIPMENT MALFUNCTIONS

15 — Systems and Equipment Malfunctions

There are some emergency conditions that do not appear in checklists or in your airplane's POH. Although these situations are not specifically addressed, the FAA provides some general recommendations for dealing with them. The procedures are not intended to be used in lieu of the particular recommendations that may be provided by a manufacturer, but rather in their absence.

In-Flight Fire

If you experience a fire while in flight, follow the checklist procedures specified in the POH for your airplane and declare an emergency by radio. The checklist may address only one type of in-flight fire or it might include procedures for different types of fires ranging from cabin and electrical fires to engine fires. In any event, follow the appropriate procedure for the situation. In addition, a general recommendation may be of benefit to you during such an emergency. Should the fire and flames be visible outside the cabin during the emergency descent, attempt to slip away from the fire as much as possible. For example, if the fire is observed on the left side of the airplane, slip to the right. This may move the fire away from the cabin.

Partial Power Loss

It is possible that during a flight you may experience a partial loss of engine power. Two options might be available to you, depending on the degree of power loss and the airplane's resulting decrease in performance. You may be able to continue the flight in a reduced power condition as long as you are able to hold altitude or climb. In this situation, maintain an airspeed that will provide the best airplane performance available. In most cases, the best performance airspeed will be approximately the best glide speed. However, it is also possible the engine will not continue to run in this condition and a forced landing will still need to be made. With an engine problem, you should continually monitor your engine instruments and update your choice of landing options.

Alternatively, your airplane's performance with partial power may not be sufficient to maintain altitude. In this case, a forced landing is imminent. Consequently, you will need to declare an emergency with ATC and begin the emergency approach and landing procedures specified in your airplane's checklist.

Door Opening in Flight

A cabin or baggage compartment door opening in flight can be a disconcerting event. Although a door generally will not open very far, the sudden noise can be startling. Regardless of the noise and confusion, it is important to maintain control of the airplane, particularly during departure. Accidents have occurred on takeoff because pilots have stopped flying the airplane to concentrate on closing cabin or baggage doors.

While an open door does not normally compromise airplane control, it is possible that control will become more difficult. If such a condition should occur it may be necessary to increase airspeed in all phases of flight, including the approach, in order to ensure that you can control the airplane. Once you have adequate airplane control, land as soon as practical and secure the door.

Asymmetrical Flap Extension

An unexpected rolling motion during flap extension may be due to an asymmetrical or split flap condition. If one flap extends while the other remains in place, a differential in lift across the wing is the cause of the rolling motion. A split flap condition can be hazardous, particularly in the traffic pattern or during a turn at low altitude.

Systems and Equipment Malfunctions

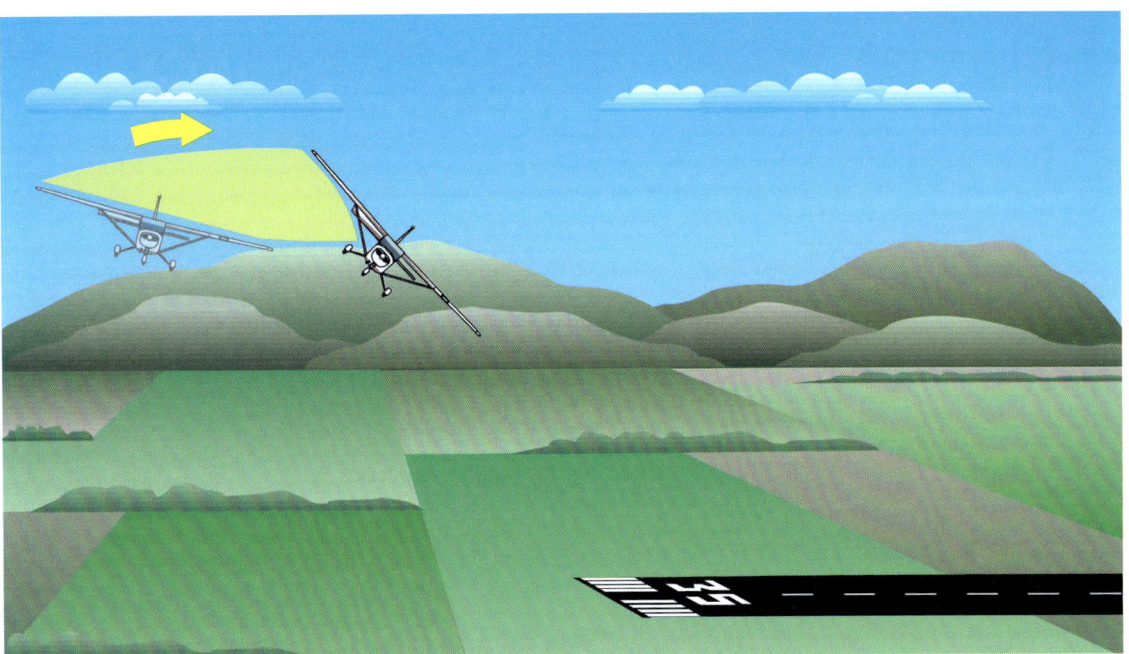

Extending the flaps during a turn can result in a dangerous situation should an asymmetrical flap extension occur. If the unexpected rolling motion occurs during flap extension, immediately return the flap control to the up, or the previous position, while maintaining control of the airplane. Should you be in the approach phase of the traffic pattern when an asymmetrical extension occurs, execute a go-around and adjust your airspeed for approach and landing.

SYSTEMS AND EQUIPMENT MALFUNCTIONS

To meet the PTS requirements, you must:

- Exhibit knowledge of the elements related to system and equipment malfunctions appropriate to the airplane provided for the practical test.

- Analyze the situation and take appropriate action for simulated emergencies appropriate to the airplane provided for the practical test for at least three (3) of the following:

    a. Partial or complete power loss.

    b. Engine roughness or overheat.

    c. Carburetor or induction icing.

    d. Loss of oil pressure.

    e. Fuel starvation.

    f. Electrical malfunction.

    g. Vacuum/pressure, and associated flight instruments malfunction.

    h. Pitot/static.

    i. Landing gear or flap malfunction.

    j. Inoperative trim.

    k. Inadvertent door or window opening.

    l. Structural icing.

    m. Smoke/fire/engine compartment fire.

    n. Any other emergency appropriate to the airplane.

- Follow the appropriate checklist or procedure.

16 — Emergency Descent

An emergency descent is a maneuver for descending as rapidly as possible to a lower altitude or to the ground for an emergency landing. The need for this maneuver may result from an uncontrollable fire, smoke in the cockpit, a sudden loss of cabin pressurization, or any other situation that demands an immediate rapid descent.

The objective is to descend the airplane as soon and as rapidly as possible, within the structural limitations of the airplane. Emergency descents should be performed as recommended by the POH, observing recommended aircraft configurations, power settings, and airspeeds. The pilot should not allow the airplane to exceed the never-exceed speed (V_{NE}), maximum landing gear extended speed (V_{LE}), maximum flap extended speed (V_{FE}), or maneuvering speed (V_A), as applicable.

When performing an emergency descent, make a radio call to alert ATC and other aircraft of your intentions. Configure the airplane, within the POH guidelines, to descend as rapidly as possible

1. Reduce the power to idle.

2. Place the propeller control (if equipped) to the low-pitch/high-rpm position.

3. Extend the landing gear and flaps, as recommended by the POH.

Bank approximately 30° to 45° to:

- Scan for other traffic below.
- Look for a possible emergency landing area.
- Increase the rate of descent.

A bank angle of approximately 30° to 45° will maintain a positive load factor on the airplane.

Descend at the maximum allowable airspeed:

- V_{NE} for a clean aircraft, with no structural damage, in smooth air.
- V_A for a clean aircraft, with no structural damage, in turbulent air.
- V_{FE} or V_{LE} whichever is more restrictive and applicable to your POH recommended aircraft configuration.

Complete the appropriate emergency descent checklist.

Level the airplane off by gradually raising the nose approximately 100 feet prior to the desired leveloff altitude.

Generally, a 10% lead is sufficient for leveloff. For example, 10% of a 1,000 fpm descent would yield a 100-foot lead for leveloff.

Reduce your airspeed, as applicable, to reconfigure the airplane.

Add power as necessary to maintain airspeed.

Emergency Descent

During training, you should terminate the procedure when the descent is stabilized and the Emergency Descent checklist is complete. In airplanes with piston engines, avoid prolonged practice of emergency descents to prevent excessive cooling of the engine cylinders.

In an actual emergency, prepare for landing using the ABC's:

   A. Get the current ATIS or weather.

   B. Brief your approach and landing requirements.

   C. Complete all required checklists.

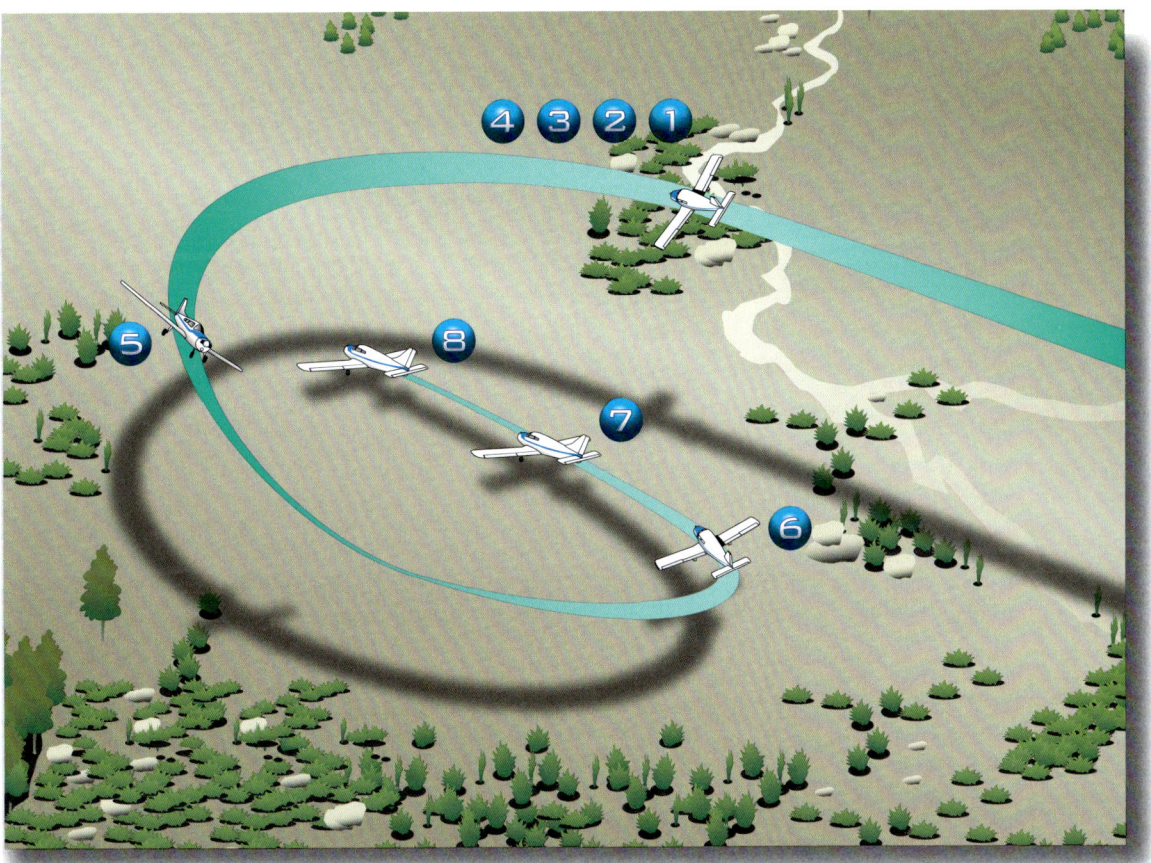

 Emergency Descent

To meet the PTS requirements, you must:

- Exhibit satisfactory knowledge of the elements related to an emergency descent.

- Recognize situations, such as depressurization, cockpit smoke, and/or fire that require an emergency descent.

- Establish the appropriate airspeed and configuration for the emergency descent.

- Exhibit orientation, division of attention, and proper planning.

- Maintain a postive load factor during the maneuver.

17 — Emergency Approach and Landing

Modern airplane engines are extremely reliable and actual mechanical malfunctions are rare. However, due to inadvertent fuel exhaustion or an engine component malfunction you could find yourself making an emergency approach and landing. Using a checklist is the best way to ensure that items are not omitted from an emergency procedure. In some cases, however, you may not have time to review or even access a checklist. To help you respond quickly to an emergency, some checklists have immediate action items printed in bold type which should be committed to memory. In addition, you should always maintain situational awareness and be constantly on the alert for suitable emergency landing fields. The following guidelines, as well as frequent practice with your flight instructor, will help you develop the ability to plan and methodically execute emergency landing procedures.

Since most practice emergency landing approaches terminate in a go-around, it is possible for you to fall into the habit of considering the procedure as just another training exercise. To avoid this, assume that each simulated emergency may actually result in a landing. The following general steps are used to cope with an emergency landing situation.

1. Maintain control of the airplane and adjust the pitch to achieve best glide speed. Once the glide speed is attained, trim to relieve control pressures and to aid in maintaining the proper attitude and airspeed.

Attaining best glide speed is an immediate action item. Normally, you will need to apply back pressure to the yoke to slow the airplane to the appropriate gliding attitude and speed. However, if your airspeed is below the best glide speed at the time of the engine failure, lower the nose immediately to obtain best glide speed and trim to relieve control pressures.

2. Scan the terrain around the airplane and select a suitable field that is within gliding distance from your present altitude.

- When selecting a field, you must consider the wind direction and speed, length of the field, obstructions, and surface condition. A long field positioned into the wind, with a firm, smooth surface that is free of obstructions is the most desirable.

- Avoid fields which have large boulders, ditches, or other landing hazards. If you choose a plowed field, the landing should be made parallel to the furrows. When considering a road, be alert for powerlines, signs, and automobile traffic.

- Evaluate your options if a field with ideal landing features is not available. For example, it may be better to accept a crosswind landing on a long field, rather than attempt to land into the wind on a very short field. On another occasion, a downwind landing with light winds and no obstructions may be preferable to a landing into the wind with numerous obstacles.

Do not limit your search for a landing field to the terrain ahead of the airplane, since you may have just flown by a field better suited for landing. In a low-wing airplane, the wing blocks the area to the right and left of the airplane so you may be required to make shallow turns to scan the area.

3. Turn toward the intended landing field.

- Dissipate any excess altitude near the field so you are in a good position to observe the field carefully for wires, fences, holes, tree stumps, or other hazards.

- A circling approach over the field allows you to make adjustments for altitude and keeps you in a position from which you can reach the field.

- Advise your passengers to fasten their seatbelts and shoulder harnesses.

Remember, turning upwind will reduce your groundspeed and glide distance. Conversely, turning downwind will increase your groundspeed and glide distance. The estimation of glide distance is difficult so it is inadvisable to circle away from the field and then try to make a long straight-in glide to the field.

Emergency Approach and Landing

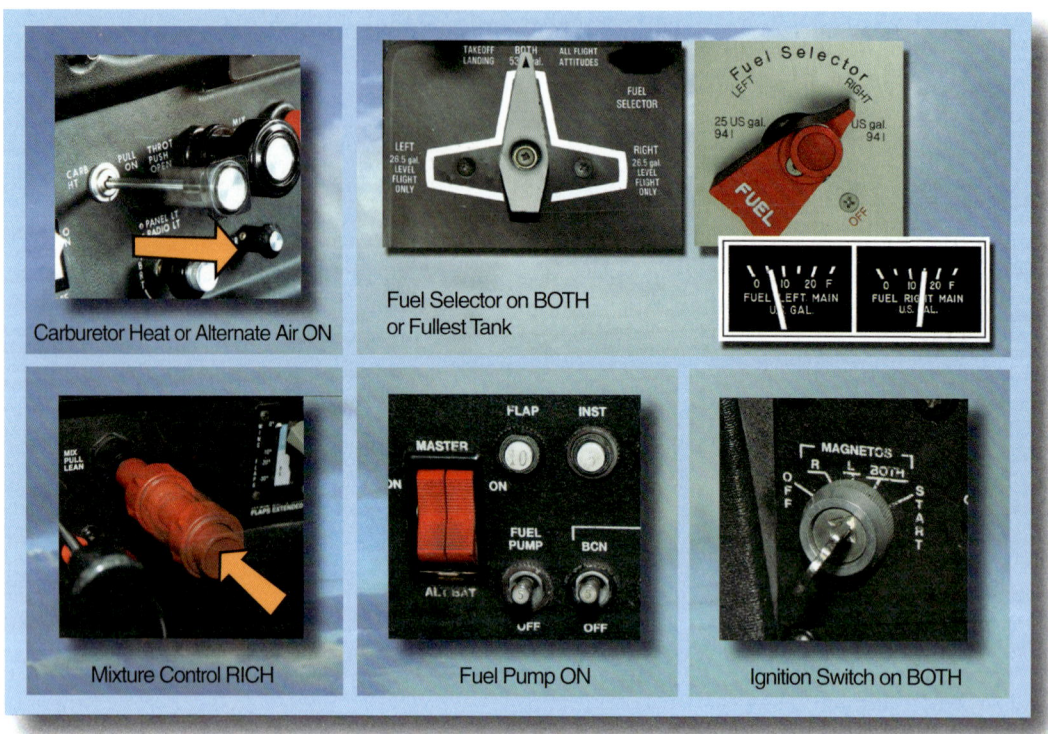

Carburetor Heat or Alternate Air ON
Fuel Selector on BOTH or Fullest Tank
Mixture Control RICH
Fuel Pump ON
Ignition Switch on BOTH

4. Follow an appropriate emergency checklist and attempt to determine the cause of the power failure. Restart the engine, if possible.

Typically, you should initially make a quick check for obvious problems, then carefully follow the appropriate emergency checklist to ensure that items are not omitted. Be methodical and perform your troubleshooting in a definite sequence.

- If applicable, place the carburetor heat control to the ON position.

- Move the fuel selector to the BOTH position or select the fullest tank.

- Adjust the mixture to the full RICH position.

- Switch the fuel pump ON (if installed).

- Check the ignition switch and select the BOTH position, or engage the starter if the propeller is stopped.

When attempting to restart the engine, you normally will not need to use the starter since the propeller usually continues to turn, or windmill, in a power-off glide.

Emergency Approach and Landing

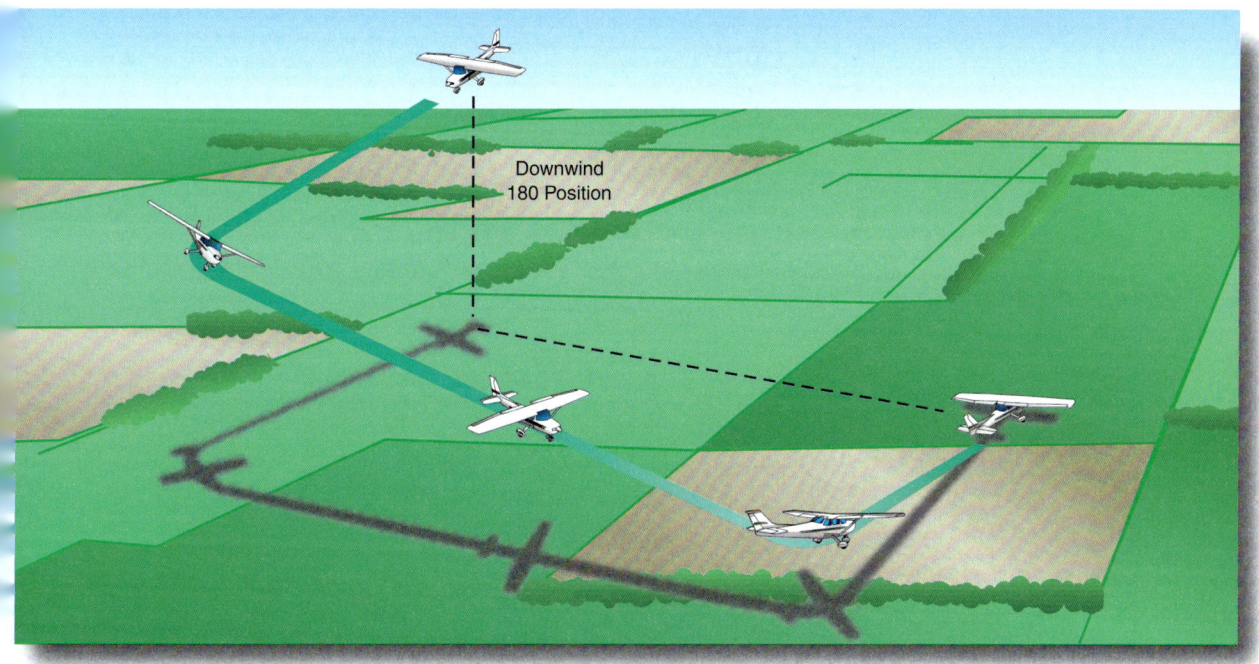

5. Set up a landing approach to the selected field. Attempt to maneuver the airplane to be at the 180° position on downwind when you reach a normal traffic pattern altitude. From this point, you can perform a normal power-off approach.

> If the altitude at which the power failure occurs is too low or the distance to a suitable landing field is too great, you may not be able to arrive at the 180° position. If this situation occurs, plan the approach so the airplane can intercept the normal traffic pattern. For example, the next best place for interception may be the key position. Keep in mind the distance traveled in the landing flare. If the desired landing point is just beyond a ditch, the aiming point must be on the near side of the ditch.

- If time permits, use your radio and declare an emergency, giving your position as accurately as possible. In addition, set your transponder to the emergency code of 7700.

6. Most POHs provide a checklist for shutting down the engine and configuring the airplane once the landing is assured. During a practice emergency landing procedure, your instructor may have you simulate performing items on the checklist.

- Set the mixture to IDLE CUT OFF.

- Move the fuel selector to the OFF position.

EMERGENCY APPROACH AND LANDING

- Turn the ignition switch to the OFF position.

> Since the flaps shorten your glide distance, they should not be lowered until you are confident of reaching the emergency landing field.

- Position the flaps as recommended by the POH.

- Toggle the master switch to the OFF position.

7. In an actual emergency landing, touch down on the main wheels first, then gently lower the nose of the airplane. Apply the brakes as required to stop the airplane. During a practice emergency landing, initiate a go-around when your instructor specifies.

EMERGENCY APPROACH AND LANDING

To meet the PTS requirements, you must:

- Exhibit knowledge of the elements related to emergency approach and landing procedures.

- Analyze the situation and select an appropriate course of action.

- Establish and maintain the recommended best-glide airspeed, +/-10 knots.

- Select a suitable landing area.

- Plan and follow a flight pattern to the selected landing area considering altitude, wind, terrain, and obstructions.

- Prepare for landing, or go-around, as specified by the examiner.

- Follow the appropriate checklist.

EXERCISES — EMERGENCY LANDING PROCEDURES

15 — SYSTEMS AND EQUIPMENT MALFUNCTIONS

1. What should you do if you experience an in-flight fire?

2. If you experience a partial power loss, what options do you have?

3. What action is advised if a door opens in flight?

4. How can you counter a sudden, unexpected rolling motion following flap extension?

5. Why should you avoid flap extension during turns in the traffic pattern?

16 — Emergency Descent

1. True/False. You control your rate of descent with airspeed. _____

2. True/False. You can decrease your descent rate by increasing drag. _____

3. During a 1000 fpm descent, you have been instructed to level off at 3,000 feet MSL. At what altitude should you begin your leveloff?

4. In smooth air, what airspeed would you perform an emergency descent if the aircraft had no flaps or landing gear extended?

5. In turbulent air, what airspeed would you perform an emergency descent if the aircraft had no flaps or landing gear extended?

EXERCISES — EMERGENCY LANDING PROCEDURES

17 — EMERGENCY APPROACH AND LANDING

1. What is the first action you should take when an engine failure occurs?
   _____

2. What are some of factors that you need to consider when selecting an appropriate field for an emergency landing?
   _____

3. True/False. When making an emergency landing, it is recommended that you circle away from the field and then execute a long straight-in approach to the landing area. _____

4. What code should you set in your transponder to indicate an emergency?
   _____

5. Why should you wait to lower the flaps until you are confident of making the landing field?
   _____

FLIGHT MANEUVERS

FLIGHT MANEUVERS

FLIGHT MANEUVERS

MANEUVER 18 5-2
   SLOW FLIGHT

MANEUVER 19 5-4
   POWER-OFF STALLS

MANEUVER 20 5-8
   POWER-ON STALLS

MANEUVER 21 5-11
   DEMONSTRATED STALLS

MANEUVER 22 5-14
   STEEP TURNS

EXERCISES............................. 5-17

Video Volume II — Flight Maneuvers, Ground Reference Maneuvers, Performance Takeoffs and Landings, and Special Flight Operations

Computer Training — Flight Maneuvers

Collision avoidance is an important safety consideration every time you fly and particularly when maneuvering your airplane in the practice area. In the practice environment you can be easily distracted so you should make a special effort to maintain your visual scan while maneuvering. Your instructor will help you with your scanning technique and encourage you to concentrate your vision outside the airplane. Your instructor also will show you how to clear the area prior to maneuvering.

Before you begin a maneuver, you should make clearing turns that usually consist of at least a 180° change in direction, such as two 90° turns. Clearing turns provide you with a view of the area around your flight path and make it easier to maintain visual contact with other aircraft in the practice area.

18 — Slow Flight

The purpose of maneuvering during slow flight is to help you develop a feel for the airplane's controls at slow airspeeds, as well as gain an understanding of how load factor, pitch attitude, airspeed, and altitude control relate to each other. Slow flight may be broadly defined as flight at an airspeed below the normal cruise speed. However, during training you will normally practice this maneuver at airspeeds well below the normal cruise speed. The speed used to demonstrate slow flight for the practical test is sufficiently slow so that any significant reduction in speed or power, or increase in load factor, results in stall indications.

While in slow flight, any change in flight attitude, such as a level turn or increase in pitch attitude, increases the airplane's load factor, as well as its stall speed. Since the airspeed is just above a stall speed during slow flight, any maneuvering should be accompanied by a corresponding change in power to prevent the aircraft from stalling. Coordinated flight is essential throughout all slow flight maneuvers.

Before beginning a slow flight maneuver, you should do a clearing turn to check for traffic. You may either execute one 180° turn or two 90° turns in opposite directions. Start the maneuver at an altitude which will allow you to recover no lower than 1,500 feet AGL. It is a good idea to select an entry altitude and heading which can be easily read on your instruments, such as 3,500 feet and 090°.

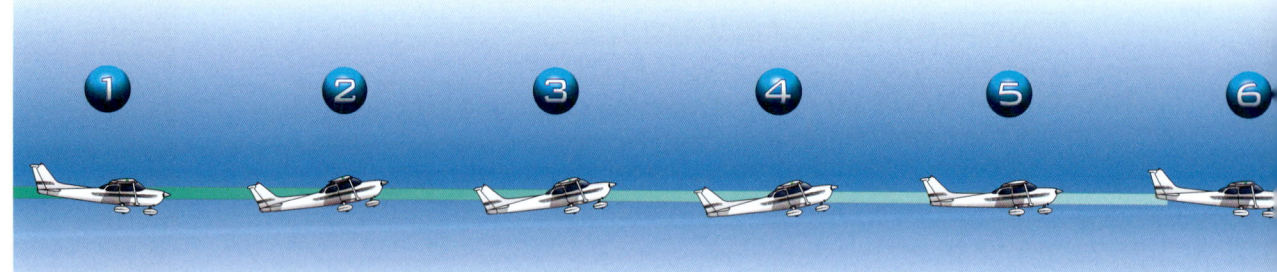

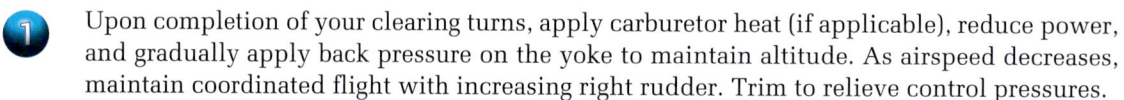
Upon completion of your clearing turns, apply carburetor heat (if applicable), reduce power, and gradually apply back pressure on the yoke to maintain altitude. As airspeed decreases, maintain coordinated flight with increasing right rudder. Trim to relieve control pressures.

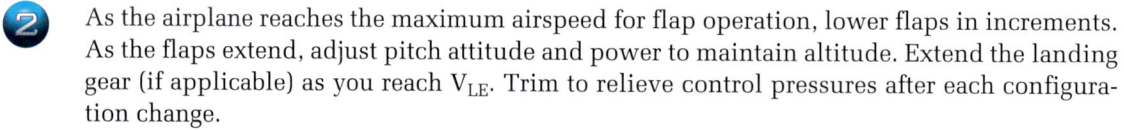
As the airplane reaches the maximum airspeed for flap operation, lower flaps in increments. As the flaps extend, adjust pitch attitude and power to maintain altitude. Extend the landing gear (if applicable) as you reach V_{LE}. Trim to relieve control pressures after each configuration change.

> To maintain coordinated flight, use right rudder to offset the left-turning tendencies associated with the low-airspeed, high-power flight regime.

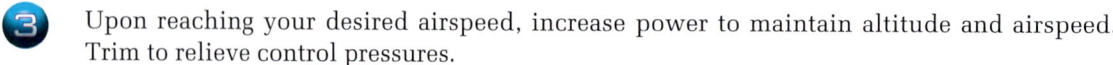
Upon reaching your desired airspeed, increase power to maintain altitude and airspeed. Trim to relieve control pressures.

Once established in slow flight, you primarily maintain airspeed and altitude by making small power adjustments as necessary. To maintain the proper pitch attitude, you should divide your attention between outside references and instrument indications. The correct procedure for regaining lost altitude is to apply power. When you do this, it will also be necessary to make a small increase in pitch attitude to maintain the desired airspeed. To lose altitude, reduce power and, at the same time, reduce pitch attitude slightly.

4. Once the airplane is stabilized, perform turns, climbs (if possible), and descents as directed by your instructor. To climb, you must coordinate a pitch and power increase to maintain airspeed. Correspondingly, a descent requires a coordinated pitch and power decrease to maintain airspeed. The shallow turns you execute during slow flight will require you to add power to maintain airspeed and avoid a stall.

When you are maneuvering during slow flight, you will get a sensation of insufficient control response. The controls feel mushy, and it is necessary to use greater control movements for corrections than are normally required.

5. When directed by your instructor, set the carburetor heat to COLD (if applicable) and add full power to return to cruise flight. While maintaining your heading and altitude, raise the flaps slowly in increments. Also, raise the landing gear (if applicable). As the airplane accelerates, lower the nose attitude and anticipate the need for less right rudder to maintain coordinated flight.

6. As you reach your desired airspeed, reduce power and trim to relieve control pressures.

MANEUVERING DURING SLOW FLIGHT

To meet the PTS requirements, you must:

- Exhibit knowledge of the elements related to maneuvering during slow flight.

- Select an entry altitude that will allow that task to be completed no lower than 1,500 feet (460 meters) AGL.

- Establish and maintain an airspeed at which any further increase in angle of attack, increase in load factor, or reduction in power, would result in an immediate stall.

- Accomplish coordinated straight-and-level flight, turns, climbs, and descents with landing gear and flap configuration specified by the examiner.

- Divide attention between airplane control and orientation.

- Maintain the specified altitude, ±100 feet (30 meters); specified heading ±10 degrees; airspeed ±0 knots; and specified angle of bank, ±10 degrees.

19 — Power-Off Stalls

Stalls are practiced with two goals in mind. One objective is to help you gain familiarity with the stall characteristics of your airplane so you can better avoid entering an inadvertent stall. The other reason for stall practice is to condition you to recover from an inadvertent stall quickly and with a minimal loss of altitude. Power-off stalls are performed in the landing configuration and are used to simulate an accidental stall during approach, therefore you normally practice power-off stalls using the airplane's normal approach speed.

As the airplane approaches a stall, the control feel is sometimes described as "mushy" or "soft" as compared to the more solid feel of the controls at cruise speed. Consequently, you must use a greater displacement of the controls to achieve the desired results. As the airplane slows you also will notice a decrease in engine sound as well as the tone and intensity of the slipstream noise. The airplane's mechanical stall warning, which may be a light, buzzer, horn, or other device, usually begins 5 to 10 knots before the stall. You may notice buffeting and further decay of control effectiveness just before the stall,.

After you become proficient in straight-and-level stall entries and recoveries, you will learn how to handle turning (up to 30° angle of bank) power-off stalls. Before you begin the maneuver, you should perform clearing turns and establish the airplane at an altitude which will allow you to recover by 1,500 feet AGL.

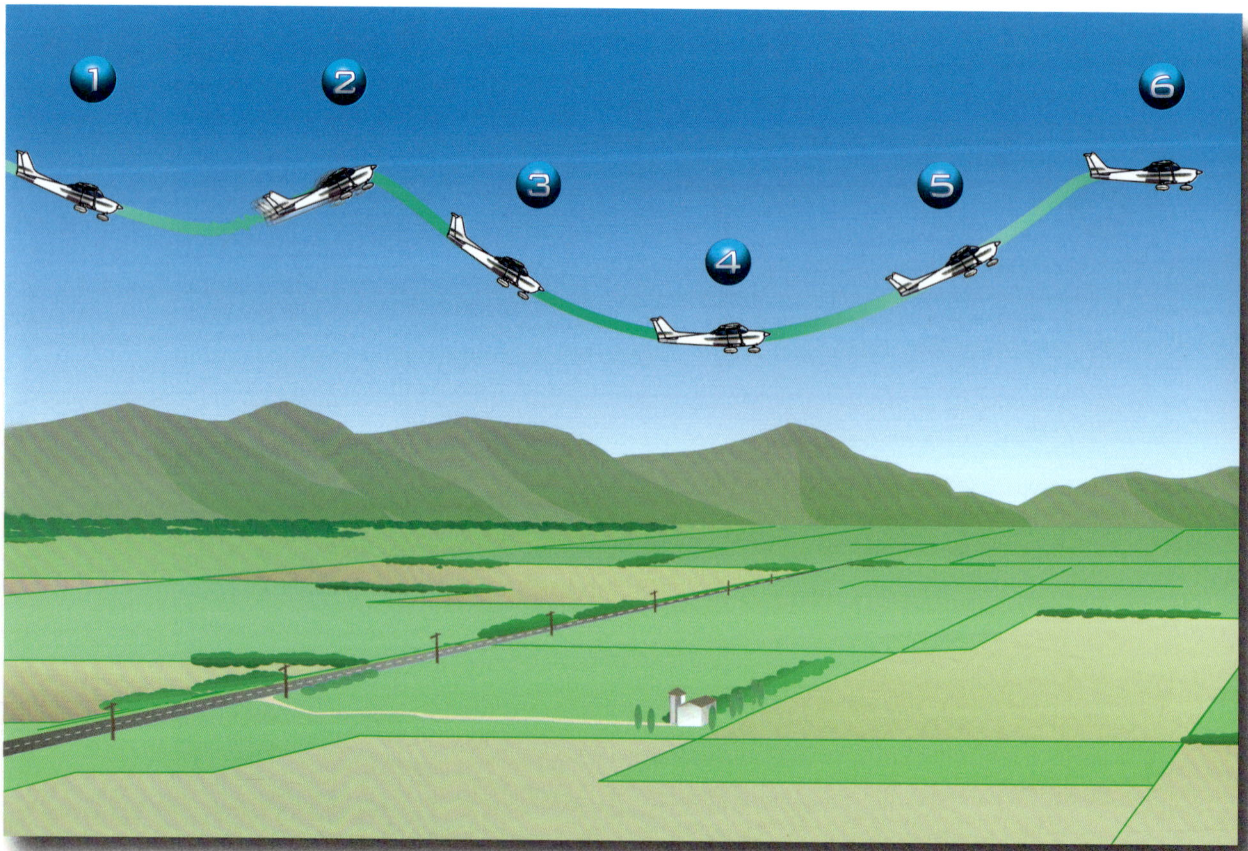

Straight-Ahead Stall

1. Upon completion of your clearing turns, apply carburetor heat (if applicable), reduce power, and gradually apply back pressure on the yoke to maintain altitude. As you reach the safe flap extension speed, lower full flaps and establish a normal glide. Extend the landing gear (if applicable). Trim to relieve control pressures.

2. Maintain coordinated flight using right rudder and apply back pressure on the yoke to raise the airplane's nose to an attitude which will induce a stall. Maintain the pitch attitude until a full stall occurs.

3. Simultaneously release back pressure, level the wings (if necessary), add full power, and set the carburetor heat to COLD (if applicable). Adjust the rudder to maintain coordinated flight. Retract the flaps to an intermediate setting.

> As the nose pitches down, the airplane may tend to roll to one side. If this occurs, use coordinated aileron and rudder pressures to level the wings at the same time you apply power and adjust the pitch attitude.

4. As flying speed is regained, adjust the pitch attitude to stop the descent and initiate a climb.

> It is important to apply the correct amount of back pressure during stall recoveries. Applying back pressure too rapidly may result in a secondary stall, while not applying it quickly enough may cause the airplane to build excessive airspeed and lose a significant amount of altitude.

5. Once you establish a positive rate of climb, retract the landing gear (if applicable). Upon reaching V_Y, retract the remainder of the flaps. Trim to relieve control pressures.

6. Upon reaching the desired altitude, level off and accelerate to the desired airspeed. Ensure you return to the proper heading, if necessary. Once you attain the proper airspeed, adjust the power and trim to relieve control pressures.

Power-Off Stalls

Turning Stall

The power-off, turning stall is a variation of the power-off straight-ahead stall. It is designed to simulate an accidental stall during a turn from base to final. Entry procedures are the same as the straight-ahead, power-off stall except with the addition of up to a 30° angle of bank.

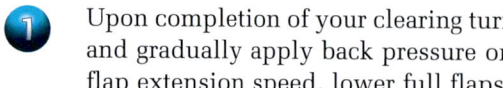

① Upon completion of your clearing turns, apply carburetor heat (if applicable), reduce power, and gradually apply back pressure on the yoke to maintain altitude. As you reach the safe flap extension speed, lower full flaps and establish a normal glide. Extend the landing gear (if applicable). Trim to relieve control pressures.

② Begin a turn to the left or right (up to 30° angle of bank). Once established in the turn, maintain coordinated flight and apply back pressure on the yoke to raise the airplane's nose to an attitude which will induce a stall.

You should not attempt to stall the airplane on a particular heading. However, to simulate the turn from base to final, the stall normally should be made to occur within 90° of turn.

③ Ensure you maintain the desired angle of bank and coordinated flight. Maintain the pitch attitude until a full stall occurs.

POWER-OFF STALLS

It is very important to maintain coordinated flight during all stalls, particularly those which incorporate a turn. If not in coordinated flight during a turning, power-off stall, the airplane may wallow when the stall occurs or, if the airplane is in a slip, the outer wing may stall first and abruptly whip downward.

4. To recover from the stall, simultaneously release back pressure, level the wings, add full power, and set the carburetor heat to COLD (if applicable). Adjust the rudder to maintain coordinated flight. Retract the flaps to an intermediate setting.

5. As flying speed is regained, adjust the pitch attitude to stop the descent and initiate a climb.

It is important to apply the correct amount of back pressure during stall recoveries. Applying back pressure too rapidly may result in a secondary stall, while not applying it quickly enough may cause the airplane to build excessive airspeed and lose a significant amount of altitude.

6. Once you establish a positive rate of climb, retract the landing gear (if applicable). Upon reaching V_Y, retract the remainder of the flaps. Trim to relieve control pressures.

7. Upon reaching the desired altitude, level off and accelerate to the desired airspeed. Ensure you return to the proper heading, if necessary. Once you attain the proper airspeed, adjust the power and trim to relieve control pressures.

POWER-OFF STALLS

To meet the PTS requirements, you must:

- Exhibit knowledge of the elements related to power-off stalls.

- Select an entry altitude that allows the task to be completed no lower than 1,500 feet (460 meters) AGL.

- Establish a stabilized descent in the approach or landing configuration, as specified by the examiner.

- Transition smoothly from the approach or landing attitude to a pitch attitude that will induce a stall.

- Maintain a specified heading, ±10 degrees, in straight flight; maintain a specified angle of bank not to exceed 20 degrees, ±10 degrees; in turning flight, while inducing the stall.

- Recognize and recover promptly after the stall occurs by simultaneously reducing the angle of attack, increasing power to maximum allowable, and leveling the wings to return to a straight-and-level flight attitude with a minimum loss of altitude appropriate for the airplane.

- Retract the flaps to the recommended setting; retract the landing gear, if retractable, after a positive rate of climb is established.

- Accelerate to V_X or V_Y speed before the final flap retraction; return to the altitude, heading, and airspeed specified by the examiner.

20 — Power-On Stalls

Power-on stalls are usually practiced from straight climbs and climbing turns to simulate an accidental stall during takeoffs and departure climbs. The straight-ahead stall can occur if you attempt to take off at too slow an airspeed and apply excessive back pressure on the yoke. This produces an extreme nose-high attitude and high angle of attack. The power-on, turning stall normally occurs during the departure turn following takeoff and results from distractions which divert your attention from flying the airplane. The indications of the approaching stall are similar to those you experience during a power-off stall (see Maneuver #18). As with all stalls, power-on stalls should be practiced at an entry altitude which permits a safe recovery no lower than 1,500 feet AGL. Normally, you will practice in the takeoff and departure configuration and at the aircraft's takeoff speed. This may involve the extension of landing gear and/or flaps, depending on the situation.

Straight-Ahead Stall

Although you use a high power setting during this stall, do not enter it from a high airspeed. An extremely nose-high pitch attitude can result from high-power, high-airspeed stall entries.

 Upon completion of your clearing turns, reduce power and slow the airplane while using back pressure on the yoke to maintain altitude.

 As you reach liftoff speed, simultaneously set takeoff power (or the recommended climb power setting) and smoothly apply back pressure on the yoke to raise the airplane's nose to an attitude which will induce a stall. Maintain the pitch attitude until a full stall occurs. Ensure you maintain coordinated flight.

Power-On Stalls

You will need increasing right rudder pressure to maintain coordinated flight as you increase the power and pitch attitude. In many airplanes, the elevator (or stabilator) may be fully deflected by the time the airplane fully stalls.

3. Simultaneously release back pressure and apply full power (if not already at full power). If flaps were lowered, retract them to an intermediate setting.

As the nose pitches down, the airplane may tend to roll to one side. If this occurs, use coordinated aileron and rudder pressures to level the wings at the same time you apply power and adjust the pitch attitude.

4. As flying speed is regained, adjust the pitch attitude to stop the descent and initiate a climb.

It is important to apply the correct amount of back pressure during stall recoveries. Applying back pressure too rapidly may result in a secondary stall, while not applying it quickly enough may cause the airplane to build excessive airspeed and lose a significant amount of altitude.

5. Once you establish a positive rate of climb, retract the landing gear (if applicable). Upon reaching V_Y, retract the remainder of the flaps. Trim to relieve control pressures.

6. Upon reaching the desired altitude, level off and accelerate to the desired airspeed. Ensure you return to the proper heading, if necessary. Once you attain the proper airspeed, adjust the power and trim to relieve control pressures.

Turning Stall

The power-on, turning stall is a variation of the power-on straight-ahead stall. Entry procedures are the same as the straight-ahead, power-on stall except with the addition of up to a 20° angle of bank.

1. Upon completion of your clearing turns, reduce power and slow the airplane while using back pressure on the yoke to maintain altitude.

2. As you approach liftoff speed, begin a turn to the left or right (up to 20° angle of bank). Once established, and upon reaching liftoff speed, simultaneously set takeoff power (or the recommended climb power setting) and smoothly apply back pressure on the yoke to raise the airplane's nose to an attitude which will induce a stall. Ensure you maintain the desired angle of bank and coordinated flight.

Power-On Stalls

As you approach the stall, the angle of bank tends to steepen in a left turn and become shallower in a right turn. This occurs because torque and P-factor tend to roll the airplane to the left.

 To recover from the stall, simultaneously release back pressure, roll wings-level using coordinated rudder and aileron pressure, and apply full power (if not already at full power). If flaps were lowered, retract them to an intermediate setting.

 As flying speed is regained, adjust the pitch attitude to stop the descent and initiate a climb.

It is important to apply the correct amount of back pressure during stall recoveries. Applying back pressure too rapidly may result in a secondary stall, while not applying it quickly enough may cause the airplane to build excessive airspeed and lose a significant amount of altitude.

5. Once you establish a positive rate of climb, retract the landing gear (if applicable). Upon reaching V_Y, retract the remainder of the flaps. Trim to relieve control pressures.

6. Upon reaching the desired altitude, level off and accelerate to the desired airspeed. Ensure you return to the proper heading, if necessary. Once you attain the proper airspeed, adjust the power and trim to relieve control pressures.

POWER-ON STALLS

To meet the PTS requirements, you must:

- Exhibit knowledge of the elements related to power-on stalls.

- Select an entry altitude that allows the task to be completed no lower than 1,500 feet (460 meters) AGL.

- Establish the takeoff or departure configuration. Set power to no less than 65 percent available power.

- Transition smoothly from the takeoff or departure attitude to the pitch attitude that will induce a stall.

- Maintain a specified heading, ±10 degrees, in straight flight; maintain a specified angle of bank not to exceed 20 degrees, ±10 degrees; in turning flight, while inducing the stall.

- Recognize and recover promptly after the stall occurs by simultaneously reducing the angle of attack, increasing power to maximum allowable, and leveling the wings to return to a straight-and-level flight attitude with a minimum loss of altitude appropriate for the airplane.

- Retract the flaps to the recommended setting; retract the landing gear, if retractable, after a positive rate of climb is established.

- Accelerate to V_X or V_Y speed before the final flap retraction; return to the altitude, heading, and air speed specified by the examiner.

21 — Demonstrated Stalls

A regulatory requirement for every recreational, private, and commercial pilot applicant includes **aeronautical knowledge** training in stall awareness, spin entry, spins, and spin recovery techniques. A thorough discussion of these topics is contained in Chapter 3, Section B of the *Private Pilot Manual*. As an applicant for a private pilot certificate, you are not required to demonstrate **flight proficiency** in spin entries, spins, or spin recovery procedures. However, your flight instructor may demonstrate a spin sometime during your private pilot training. Spins should never be attempted without an experienced instructor on board. Demonstrated ability to perform power-off and power-on stalls are required for private pilot certification, whereas secondary, accelerated maneuver stalls, crossed-control stalls, and elevator trim stalls may only be demonstrated by your instructor and only if your airplane is certificated for these types of operations. The procedures contained in the following discussion are only presented so you can more completely understand how and why the stalls occur and how the associated recovery should be accomplished. You should never practice these maneuvers solo.

Secondary Stalls

A secondary stall is caused by trying to recover from a stall before the airplane has obtained sufficient flying speed. This type of stall also may occur if you attempt to return to straight-and-level flight prematurely during a spin recovery. The objective of demonstrating a secondary stall is to show you how to recognize the characteristics of the stall and the correct methods of recovery. After clearing turns, your instructor will start the demonstration using the listed procedures at an altitude that will ensure a safe recovery no lower than 1,500 feet AGL.

1. Execute a normal power-on or power-off stall.

2. During recovery from the stall, quickly increase the pitch attitude again while maintaining directional control with aileron and rudder pressure. Allow the airplane to enter the secondary stall.

3. Recover from the secondary stall by releasing back pressure on the yoke to lower the nose. Simultaneously, increase power (if not already at full power).

4. Return to straight-and-level, coordinated flight.

Accelerated Maneuver Stall

An accelerated maneuver, or excessive back pressure, stall occurs at a higher-than-normal airspeed in steep turns, pullups, or other abrupt changes in your flight attitude. The stalls which occur from these types of maneuvers tend to develop faster than normal unaccelerated stalls. The objective of demonstrating accelerated maneuver stalls is to show you how to recognize the characteristics leading up to the stall and correct methods of recovery. It is important to recover at the first indication of the stall. A prolonged stall, with excessive airspeed may lead to a spin. After clearing turns, your instructor will start the demonstration using the listed procedures at an altitude that will ensure a safe recovery no lower than 1,500 feet AGL.

DEMONSTRATED STALLS

1. Establish straight-and-level flight at V_A or less.

2. Roll into a 45° angle of bank level turn while gradually increasing back pressure to maintain altitude.

3. Once the turn and bank are established, slowly increase back pressure while maintaining altitude until the airplane stalls.

4. When the airplane stalls, recover immediately by releasing back pressure on the yoke and increasing power. If the turn is not coordinated, one wing may drop suddenly, causing the airplane to roll in that direction. If this occurs, the excessive back pressure must be released to break the stall before the addition of power.

5. Return to straight-and-level, coordinated flight.

CROSSED-CONTROL STALLS

A crossed-control stall is most likely to occur during a poorly planned and executed base to final approach turn. Often this is the result of overshooting the extended runway centerline during the turn. Typically, this happens when you apply aileron pressure in one direction, rudder pressure in the opposite direction, and use excessive elevator (or stabilator) back pressure. An example is when you attempt to increase the rate of turn with rudder and back pressure while trying to keep the bank angle from steepening with the use of ailerons. In a crossed-control stall, the airplane often stalls with little warning. The nose may pitch down, the inside wing may suddenly drop, and the airplane may continue to roll to an inverted attitude. This is usually the beginning of a spin which is very dangerous at lower altitudes. It is important that this type of stall does not occur during an actual approach to a landing, since a safe recovery may be impossible due to the amount of altitude needed. After clearing turns, your instructor will start the demonstration using the listed procedures at an altitude that ensures a safe recovery no lower than 1,500 feet AGL.

1. Slowly reduce power and extend the landing gear (if applicable).

2. Continue reducing the power to IDLE.

3. Maintain altitude until a normal glide speed is reached.

4. Establish a normal glide and trim to relieve control pressures.

5. Once established in the descent, roll into a medium bank turn. During the turn, apply heavy rudder pressure in the direction of the turn. Maintain the bank by applying opposite aileron pressure. As you do so, increase back pressure on the yoke to keep the nose from lowering.

6. Increase all flight control pressures until the airplane stalls.

7. When the stall occurs, release the control pressures. If necessary, allow the roll to continue until the airplane reaches upright and level flight.

8. Increase power to maintain straight-and-level flight.

ELEVATOR TRIM STALLS

The elevator trim stall is a maneuver that demonstrates what can happen when full power is applied during a go-around and positive control of the airplane has not been established. This can happen during a normal landing approach, a simulated forced landing approach, or immediately after take-off. The objective of the demonstration is to show the recovery procedures for overcoming strong trim forces and how to maintain control of the airplane by using proper and timely trim techniques. The approaching stall should be recognized immediately and prompt recovery procedures should be implemented to prevent the stall. It is important that a power-on stall not occur from an actual go-around because the amount of pitch change and altitude required for a safe recovery may not be available. After clearing turns, your instructor will start the demonstration using the listed procedures at an altitude that ensures a safe recovery no lower than 1,500 feet AGL.

1. Slowly reduce power and extend the landing gear (if applicable).

2. Lower one-half to full flaps.

3. Continue reducing the power to IDLE.

4. Maintain altitude until normal glide speed is reached.

5. Establish a normal glide and trim the nose up to simulate a landing approach.

6. Once established in the simulated final approach glide, apply full power to simulate a go-around. The combined forces of power, engine torque, and back elevator (or stabilator) trim will make the nose pitch up sharply with a left-turning tendency. As the pitch attitude increases to a point well above the normal climb attitude, the potential for a stall exists.

7. To recover from the approaching stall, apply positive forward pressure on the yoke to lower the nose and return to a normal climbing attitude.

8. Trim to relieve excessive control pressure.

9. Continue normal go-around procedures and level off at the desired altitude.

> **SPIN AWARENESS**
>
> When studying stalls and spins, you should not only refer to the information contained in this manual, but you should also consult Chapter 3, Section B of the *Private Pilot Manual.* The PTS requires you to explain:
>
> - Aerodynamic factors related to spins.
>
> - Flight situations where unintentional spins may occur.
>
> - Procedures for recovery from unintentional spins.

22 — STEEP TURNS

A steep turn is a high performance maneuver which is usually conducted in either direction with an angle of bank of 45°, ±5°. Due to high load factors, these turns should be accomplished at an airspeed that does not exceed the airplane's maneuvering speed (V_A). The objective of performing steep turns is to develop smoothness, coordination, orientation, division of attention, and control techniques. It is a good idea to use section lines or prominent landmarks to aid in orientation. As with most flight maneuvers, you should select an entry altitude which will allow you to perform the maneuver no lower than 1,500 feet AGL.

1. Upon completion of your clearing turns, select a reference point on the horizon and note your heading and altitude.

2. Roll into a 45° angle of bank turn at or below V_A. During roll-in, smoothly add power and slowly increase back pressure on the yoke to maintain altitude. Maintain coordinated flight and trim to relieve control pressures.

> As you enter the turn, establish the bank at a moderate rate. If you roll the airplane too rapidly, you may have difficulty establishing the pitch attitude necessary to maintain altitude. Do not apply too much back pressure while initially entering the turn or you will gain altitude. However, as you become established in the turn, greater back pressure will be needed to maintain altitude.

3. Maintain your angle of bank and altitude. Confirm your attitude by referring to both the natural horizon and attitude indicator. Use your altimeter and vertical speed indicator to determine if changes in pitch are required.

STEEP TURNS

If you are losing altitude in the turn, decrease the angle of bank first, then increase back pressure on the yoke to raise the nose. Once you regain your desired altitude, roll back to the desired angle of bank.

 4 Anticipate the roll-out by leading the roll-out heading by approximately 20°. Roll out on the entry heading and altitude. During roll-out, gradually decrease back pressure on the yoke and reduce power to maintain altitude and airspeed. Trim to relieve control pressures.

During steep turns, you will encounter an overbanking tendency which is less apparent in right turns than it is in left turns. This is because torque and P-factor tend to roll the aircraft to the left and work against the overbanking tendency during a right turn. Generally, you will need more rudder and aileron pressure during the roll-out than you needed during the roll-in. This is because the control pressures exerted during the roll-out must overcome the airplane's overbanking tendency.

 **STEEP TURNS**

To meet the PTS requirements, you must:

- Exhibit knowledge of the elements related to steep turns.

- Establish the manufacturer's recommended airspeed or if one is not stated, a safe airspeed not to exceed V_A.

- Roll into a coordinated 360 degree turn; maintain a 45 degree bank.

- Perform the task in the opposite direction, as specified by the examiner.

- Divide attention between airplane control and orientation.

- Maintain the entry altitude, ±100 feet (30 meters), airspeed, ±10 knots, bank, ±5 degrees; and roll out on the entry heading, ±10 degrees.

EXERCISES — FLIGHT MANEUVERS

18 — SLOW FLIGHT

1. What speed should you maintain during slow flight?

2. What is the minimum AGL altitude you should plan to recover from slow flight?

3. True/False. As your airspeed decreases you should anticipate the need for increasing right rudder pressure. _____

4. When recovering from slow flight, what technique should you use to raise the flaps?

5. What are the performance standards for maneuvering during slow flight?

19 — POWER-OFF STALLS

1. In what airplane configuration are power-off stalls performed?

2. When does a typical mechanical stall warning activate?

3. What are the indications that a stall has occurred?

4. What is the cause of a secondary stall?

5. True/False. After recovering from a stall, you should climb at V_X. _____

20 — POWER-ON STALLS

1. In which phase(s) of flight would a power-on stall most likely occur?

2. How should the airplane be configured when performing a power-on stall?

3. True/False. You should execute a power-on stall at a high airspeed using high power. _____

4. As you approach a power-on stall in a right turn, will the angle of bank tend to increase or decrease? _____

5. What is the maximum angle of bank you should use in a turning, power-on stall? _____

Exercises — Flight Maneuvers

21 — Demonstrated Stalls

1. True/False. An applicant for a private pilot certificate is required to demonstrate flight proficiency with regard to stalls and spins. _____

2. True/False. A private pilot applicant must be able to demonstrate flight proficiency in elevator trim stalls. _____

3. True/False. Any airplane can be used to perform an accelerated stall. _____

4. What is another name for an accelerated maneuver stall?
   _____

5. When is a crossed-control stall likely to occur?
   _____

22 — Steep Turns

1. What angle of bank is normally used for steep turns? _____

2. Is overbanking tendency more apparent in a right or left turn? _____

3. How should you correct for a loss of altitude during a steep turn?
   _____

4. How much should you lead your roll-out from a steep turn? _____

5. True/False. In comparison to the roll-in, you need more rudder and aileron pressure during the roll-out from a steep turn. _____

GROUND REFERENCE MANEUVERS

GROUND REFERENCE MANEUVERS

GROUND REFERENCE MANEUVERS

MANEUVER 23 6-2
  RECTANGULAR COURSE

MANEUVER 24 6-4
  S-TURNS

MANEUVER 25 6-6
  TURNS AROUND A POINT

EXERCISES 6-9

Video Volume II — Flight Maneuvers, Ground Reference Maneuvers, Performance Takeoffs and Landings, and Special Flight Operations

Computer Training — Ground Reference Maneuvers

Since the ground reference maneuvers you are going to learn during your flight training are practiced at relatively low altitude, you should always be vigilant for appropriate emergency landing sites. Good choices for emergency landing sites might be open pastures, turf farms, and hard-packed dirt fields. A road is not always a good option because some may have power lines, trees, or heavy traffic.

23 — Rectangular Course

The objective of the rectangular course is to help you develop the skill to compensate for effects of the wind and fly a uniform traffic pattern by visual reference to the ground. This maneuver requires you to combine several flight techniques. First, you may need to use varying crab angles throughout the straight flight segments. Second, you must track an imaginary line parallel to a fixed line. Third, you need to plan ahead and use different angles of bank in order to roll out of the turns at the proper distance from the field boundary. Finally, you must maintain a constant altitude throughout the maneuver. To help you accomplish these tasks, do not forget to maintain coordinated flight and trim to relieve control pressures, as needed.

Before starting the maneuver, select a field away from a populated area which is bounded on four sides by section lines or roads. The field should have sides between one-half and one mile in length. If possible, the wind should be blowing parallel to the long side of the rectangle. Clear the area for traffic and check to ensure there are no obstructions such as towers or power lines. Also, select an emergency landing area within gliding distance. The pattern is typically flown using left turns (although you should also practice right-hand patterns) and at a distance of approximately one-quarter to one-half mile outside the field boundary. If you fly too close to the boundaries, your angle of bank in the turns will be excessive (greater than 45°) and you may have difficulty keeping the edges of the field in sight.

1. Enter the maneuver at a 45° angle to the downwind leg, at an altitude of 600 to 1,000 feet AGL. Fly parallel to the field boundary.

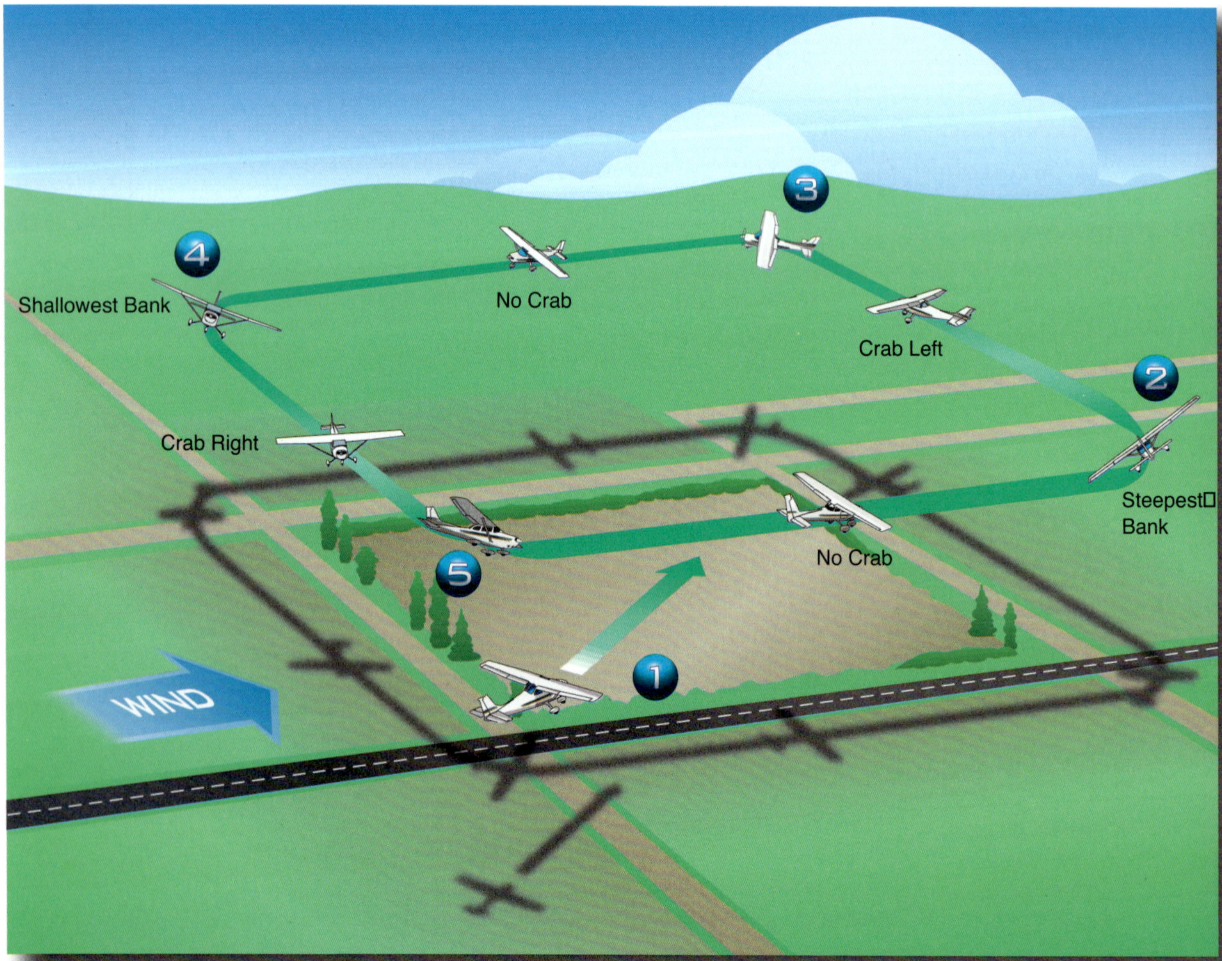

Rectangular Course

To fly a precise course, it is important that you accurately estimate the wind direction before starting the maneuver. While you can use the direction of the wind at your departure airport as a guide, you should check for other signs of wind direction near your selected field. These indicators include blowing trees, smoke, and dust, as well as advancing wave patterns on water and grain fields. You also can gain valuable information about the wind by flying a 360° constant airspeed, constant angle of bank turn.

 When you are abeam the crosswind segment of the field boundary, begin a turn to the crosswind leg. To counteract the effect of the wind and remain parallel to the crosswind field boundary, you should continue the turn beyond 90°.

The amount of bank you use is a function of groundspeed; the greater the groundspeed, the greater the angle of bank required. Since a tailwind provides the greatest groundspeed, the turn from the downwind to the crosswind leg will require the steepest angle of bank of any of the four turns. As you proceed through the first turn, your groundspeed decreases. Therefore, you should gradually decrease your angle of bank as the turn progresses. Once established on the crosswind leg, adjust the crab angle as necessary to maintain the proper distance from the field boundary.

 When you are abeam the upwind segment of the field boundary, begin a turn to the upwind leg. Since you were holding a crab angle into the wind on the crosswind leg, your turn to the upwind leg will be less than 90°.

With the increasing headwind and decreasing groundspeed, you should progressively decrease your angle of bank as the turn progresses.

 When you are abeam the next crosswind segment of the field boundary, begin a turn to the crosswind leg. To counteract the effect of wind and remain parallel to the crosswind field boundary, you should turn less than 90°.

The turn from upwind to crosswind requires the shallowest angle of bank. As the headwind component decreases, you should gradually increase your angle of bank as the turn progresses. Once established on the crosswind leg, adjust your crab angle as necessary to maintain the proper distance from the field boundary.

 When you are abeam the downwind segment of the field boundary, begin a turn to the downwind leg. Since you were holding a crab angle to compensate for the crosswind, you will need to turn greater than 90° to parallel the downwind field boundary.

With the increasing tailwind and groundspeed, you should progressively increase your angle of bank as the turn progresses.

 **RECTANGULAR COURSE**

To meet the PTS requirements, you must:

- Exhibit knowledge of the elements related to a rectangular course.

- Select a suitable reference area.

- Plan the maneuver so as to enter a left or right pattern, 600 to 1,000 feet AGL (180 to 300 meters) at an appropriate distance from the selected reference area, 45 degrees to the downwind leg.

- Apply adequate wind-drift correction during straight-and-turning flight to maintain a constant ground track around the rectangular reference area.

- Divide attention between airplane control and the ground track while maintaining coordinated flight.

- Maintain altitude, ±100 feet (30 meters); maintain airspeed, ±10 knots.

24 — S-Turns

An S-turn is a ground reference maneuver which is intended to help you improve your ability to compensate for wind drift during turns. It consists of a series of uniform 180° turns in opposite directions crossing and recrossing a straight road, fence line, or section line. The maneuver requires you to divide your attention between the ground reference line and airplane control. When selecting your ground reference, the road, fence line, or section line should be long enough to allow a series of turns. Since this maneuver should be started on a downwind heading, try to find a ground reference line which is oriented perpendicular to the wind. Clear the area for traffic and check to ensure there are no obstructions such as towers or power lines. You should fly the maneuver at an altitude low enough to easily recognize wind drift, but not any lower than 500 feet above the highest obstruction. As with most ground reference maneuvers which are performed at an altitude of between 600 to 1,000 feet AGL, you should select an emergency landing area within gliding distance prior to starting the maneuver. While flying the maneuver, maintain coordinated flight and trim to relieve control pressures, as needed.

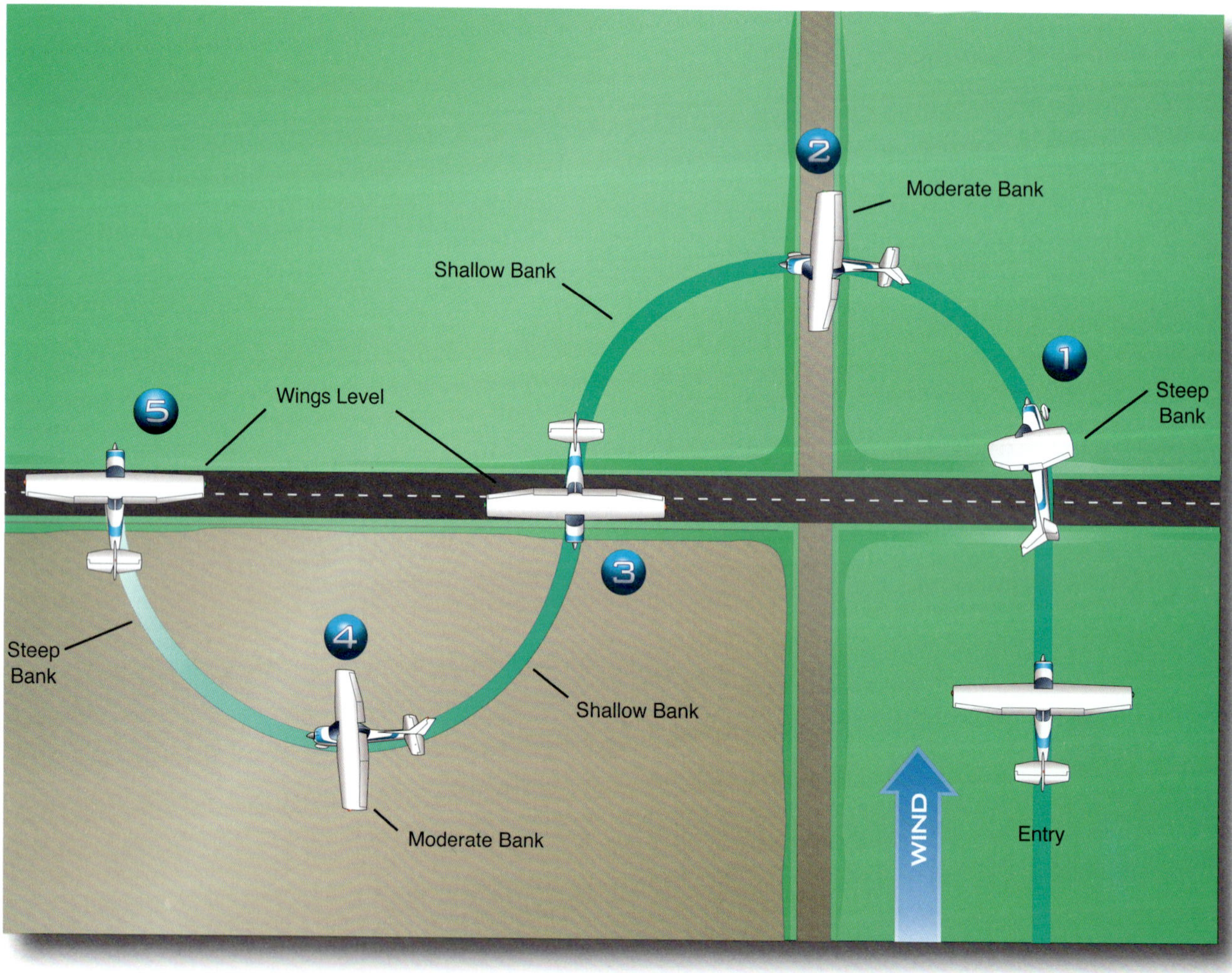

 Upon crossing the reference line, roll immediately into a left turn. The downwind entry provides the highest groundspeed in the first 90° of turn. This requires a rapid roll into a relatively steep angle of bank.

 Continue the turn, adjusting the angle of bank to compensate for the effect of the wind. As you turn past the 90° point, the airplane's groundspeed begins to decrease, requiring you to progressively reduce the angle of bank to track a symmetrical half-circle.

S - TURNS

3. You should cross the reference line after 180° of turn with the wings level. At the instant you cross the reference line, begin a turn in the opposite direction.

> There is often a tendency to increase the angle of bank too rapidly during the initial part of the turn on the upwind side, which will prevent the completion of 180° of turn before recrossing the reference line. To avoid this error, you should visualize your ground track and remember that a slow groundspeed requires a shallower angle of bank and, conversely, a high groundspeed necessitates a steeper angle of bank.

4. Continue the turn, adjusting the angle of bank to compensate for the effect of wind. As you turn past the 90° point, the airplane's groundspeed begins to increase, requiring you to progressively increase the angle of bank to track a symmetrical half-circle.

5. You should cross the reference line after the second 180° of turn with the wings level.

S-TURNS

To meet the PTS requirements, you must:

- Exhibit knowledge of the elements related to S-turns.

- Select a suitable ground reference line.

- Plan the maneuver so as to enter at 600 to 1,000 feet AGL (180 to 300 meters) AGL, perpendicular to the selected reference line.

- Apply adequate wind-drift correction during straight-and-turning flight to maintain a constant ground track around the selected reference line.

- Divide attention between airplane control and the ground track while maintaining coordinated flight.

- Maintain altitude, ±100 feet (30 meters); maintain airspeed, ±10 knots.

25 — Turns Around A Point

Turns around a point are intended to help you develop the ability to control the airplane while dividing your attention between the flight path and a ground reference point. During the maneuver, you are required to maintain a constant radius turn around a reference point while remaining at a constant altitude. The ground reference point you select should be easily identifiable, away from populated areas, and within gliding distance of a suitable emergency landing field. You can use trees, isolated haystacks, or other small landmarks as reference points, but they are not as effective as the intersections of roads or fence lines. The latter items are more desirable, because the wing may momentarily block your view of the reference point during the maneuver. By selecting a road or fence line intersection, you can mentally project these lines to their logical intersection and maintain your orientation. You should plan to begin the maneuver from a downwind entry at 600 feet to 1,000 feet AGL. The turns are initially executed to the left and normally should not exceed a 45° angle of bank.

If any wind exists, a constantly changing angle of bank will be required to maintain a uniform radius around a point. The closer the airplane is to a direct downwind heading where the groundspeed is the greatest, the steeper the bank required. Conversely, the more nearly the airplane is to a direct upwind heading where the groundspeed is least, the shallower the bank required. As always, you should maintain coordinated flight and trim to relieve control pressures, as needed, throughout the maneuver.

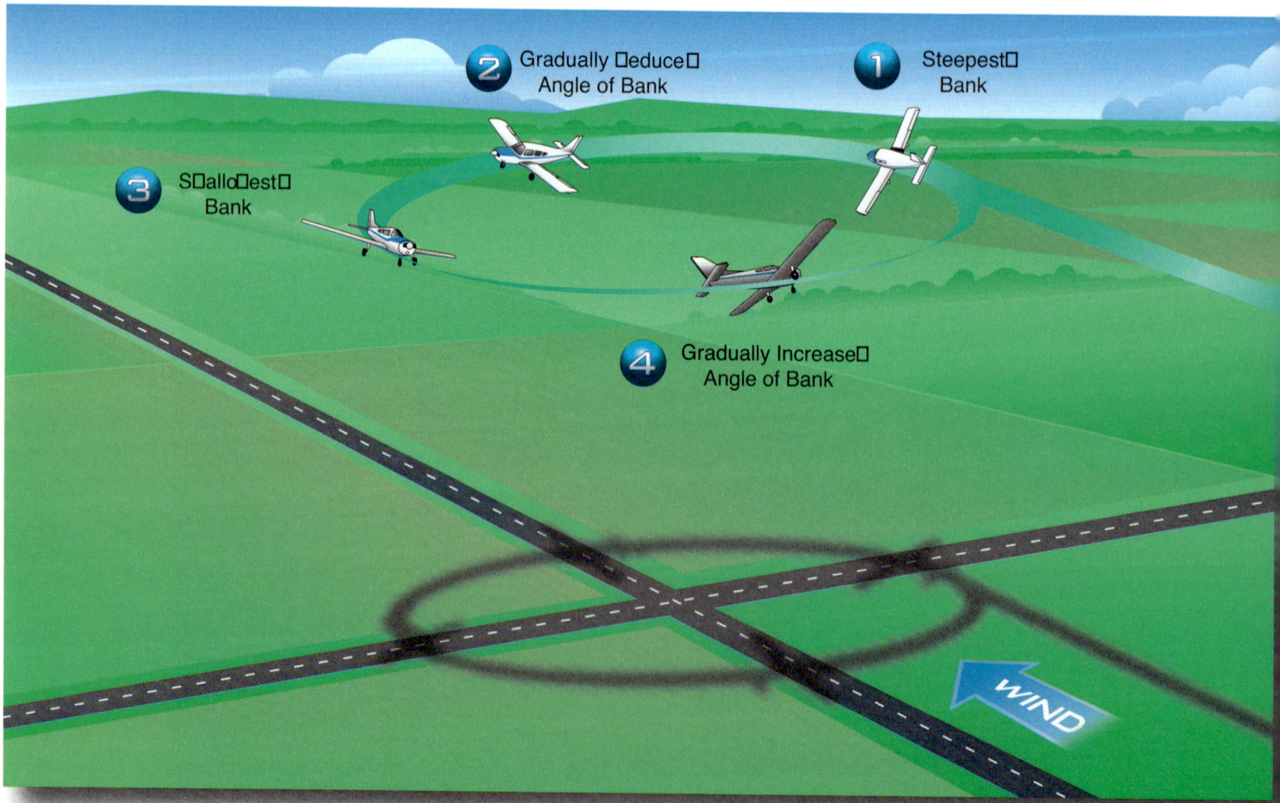

TURNS AROUND A POINT

 When the reference point is abeam the airplane on the downwind heading, roll to the left to begin the maneuver. Flying a downwind entry provides the highest groundspeed and requires the steepest initial angle of bank.

Be sure to allow the proper lateral distance between your position and the reference point. Failure to do so may result in the airplane's wing blocking your view of the reference point.

 As you turn crosswind, gradually reduce the angle of bank to compensate for the decreasing tailwind.

 Heading upwind, your bank angle will be at its shallowest due to the slow groundspeed.

When heading directly upwind, you normally will be at or near level flight.

 As you turn crosswind, gradually increase the angle of bank to maintain a uniform ground track.

 **TURNS AROUND A POINT**

To meet the PTS requirements, you must:

- Exhibit knowledge of the elements related to turns around a point.

- Select a suitable ground reference point.

- Plan the maneuver so as to enter at 600 to 1,000 feet AGL (180 to 300 meters) AGL, at an appropriate distance from the reference point.

- Apply adequate wind-drift correction to track a constant radius turn around the selected reference point.

- Divide attention between airplane control and the ground track while maintaining coordinated flight.

- Maintain altitude, ±100 feet (30 meters); maintain airspeed, ±10 knots.

EXERCISES — GROUND REFERENCE MANEUVERS

23 — RECTANGULAR COURSE

1. What other maneuver does the rectangular course simulate?

2. True/False. When you select an area to perform a rectangular course, you should also select an emergency landing field which is within gliding distance. _____

3. What is the maximum angle of bank you should use when performing a rectangular course?

4. When should you begin your turn from the downwind leg to the crosswind leg?

5. Relative to angle of bank, which turn should be the shallowest when flying a rectangular course?

24 — S-TURNS

1. During S-turns, how should the ground reference line be oriented with regard to the wind direction?

2. True/False. To begin an S-turn, you should roll into a relatively shallow bank as you cross the ground reference line. _____

3. When you turn from a downwind heading to an upwind heading, how will your groundspeed change?

4. Why should you change your angle of bank when turning from a tailwind to a headwind?

5. True/False. The ground track of the S-turn should be the same size on the upwind side as the ground track on the downwind side. _____

EXERCISE - GROUND REFERENCE MANEUVERS

25
— TURNS AROUND A POINT

1. In which direction should you initially begin your turns around a point?

2. What is the maximum angle of bank normally used when flying turns around a point?

3. When flying turns around a point, where does the steepest angle of bank occur?

4. When flying turns around a point, where does the shallowest angle of bank occur?

5. How many feet can you deviate from your entry altitude during turns around a point and still meet the PTS requirements?

PERFORMANCE TAKEOFFS & LANDINGS

PERFORMANCE TAKEOFFS & LANDINGS

PERFORMANCE TAKEOFFS AND LANDINGS

MANEUVER 26 7-2
   SHORT-FIELD TAKEOFF AND CLIMB

MANEUVER 27 7-4
   SHORT-FIELD APPROACH AND LANDING

MANEUVER 28 7-6
   SOFT-FIELD TAKEOFF AND CLIMB

MANEUVER 29 7-8
   SOFT-FIELD APPROACH AND LANDING

EXERCISES............................... 7-11

Video Volume II — Flight Maneuvers, Ground Reference Maneuvers, Performance Takeoffs and Landings, and Special Flight Operations

26 — Short-Field Takeoff And Climb

Short-field takeoff and climb procedures may be required when the usable runway length is short, or when the runway available for takeoff is restricted by obstructions, such as trees, powerlines, or buildings, at the departure end. During short-field practice sessions, it is usually assumed that you are departing from a short runway and that you must clear an obstacle which is 50 feet in height. To accomplish successful short-field takeoffs and climbs you must be familiar with the best angle-of-climb speed (V_X) and the best rate-of-climb speed (V_Y) for your airplane's. Many manufacturers also specify a best obstacle clearance speed. You should consult your airplane's POH for the appropriate speeds and specific procedures for performing short-field takeoffs. Since the same general procedures used to execute a normal takeoff and climb apply to this discussion, only the additional techniques required to perform a takeoff and climb from a short runway are explained here.

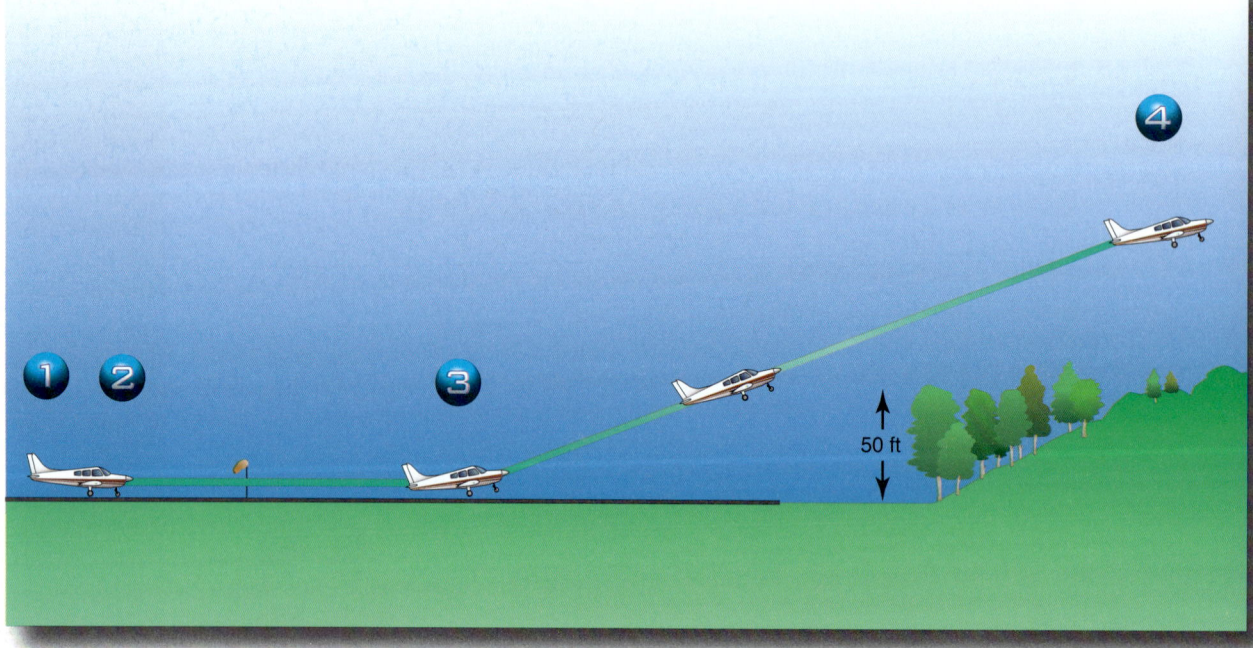

1. Complete the before takeoff check. Ensure that the runway, as well as the approach and departure paths are clear of other aircraft. After obtaining a clearance (at a controlled airport) or self announcing your intentions (at an uncontrolled airport), taxi into position at the beginning of the runway so as to allow maximum utilization of the available runway. Align the airplane on the runway centerline.

2. Set the flaps as recommended by the manufacturer. The appropriate flap setting varies between airplanes and can range from no flaps to approximately one-half flaps. While holding the brakes, add full power smoothly and continuously and then release the brakes to begin the takeoff roll.

> Holding the brakes until you achieve full power enables you to determine that the engine is functioning properly before you take off from a field where power availability is critical and distance to abort a takeoff is limited.

SHORT-FIELD TAKEOFF AND CLIMB

 3 Allow the airplane to accelerate with its full weight on the main wheels by holding the yoke to maintain the elevator (or stabilator) in a neutral position. Smoothly and firmly apply back pressure to the yoke to liftoff at the recommended airspeed. Since the airplane accelerates quickly after liftoff, you may need to apply additional back pressure to establish and maintain V_X (or best obstacle clearance speed).

> Avoid raising the nose prior to the recommended liftoff speed. A premature nose-high attitude produces drag and results in a longer takeoff roll. If you attempt to lift the airplane off the runway prematurely, or to climb too steeply, the airplane may settle back to the runway. In addition, a stall may result or the airplane may impact the obstacle.

 4 Once you have cleared the obstacle and reached a safe altitude, lower the nose and accelerate to V_Y. Retract the landing gear (if applicable) and then retract the flaps (if applicable). If no obstacles are present during training, you should maintain V_X until you are at least 50 feet above the runway surface. Trim to relieve control pressures.

> To avoid a sudden loss of lift and settling of the airplane, retract the flaps in increments.

 **SHORT-FIELD TAKEOFF AND MAXIMUM PERFORMANCE CLIMB**

To meet the PTS requirements, you must:

- Exhibit knowledge of the elements related to a short-field takeoff and maximum performance climb.
- Position the flight controls for the existing wind conditions; set the flaps as recommended.
- Clear the area; taxi into takeoff position utilizing maximum available takeoff area and align the airplane on the runway center/takeoff path.
- Apply brakes (if appropriate), while advancing the throttle smoothly to takeoff power.
- Lift off at the recommended airspeed, and accelerate to the recommended obstacle clearance airspeed or V_X.
- Establish a pitch attitude that will maintain the recommended obstacle clearance airspeed, or V_X, +10/–5 knots, until the obstacle is cleared, or until the airplane is 50 feet (20 meters) above the surface.
- After clearing the obstacle, establish the pitch attitude for V_Y, accelerate to V_Y, and maintain V_Y, +10/–5 knots, during the climb.
- Retract the landing gear, if appropriate, and flaps after clear of any obstacles or as recommended by the manufacturer.
- Maintain takeoff power to a safe maneuvering altitude.
- Maintain directional control and proper wind-drift correction throughout the takeoff and climb.
- Complete the appropriate checklist.

27 — SHORT-FIELD APPROACH AND LANDING

A short-field landing is necessary when you have a relatively short landing area or when an approach must be made over obstacles which limit the available landing area. A short-field landing consists of a steep approach over an obstacle, using power and flaps (normally full flaps). A minimum landing speed is desired with a touchdown point as close to the threshold as possible. During short-field landing practice, assume you are making the approach and landing over a 50-foot obstacle. You should consult your airplane's POH for the appropriate speeds and specific procedures for performing short-field takeoffs. Since the same general procedures used to execute a normal approach and landing apply to this discussion, only the additional techniques required to perform a short-field approach and landing are explained here.

APPROACH

1 Ensure that the before landing checklist is completed and that the area is clear. Extend approximately one-third of the available flaps during the latter portion of the downwind leg and two-thirds on base, while progressively reducing the airspeed. Trim to relieve control pressures.

2 Begin the final approach at least 500 feet higher than the touchdown area. Maintain the recommended approach speed and extend the remaining flaps.

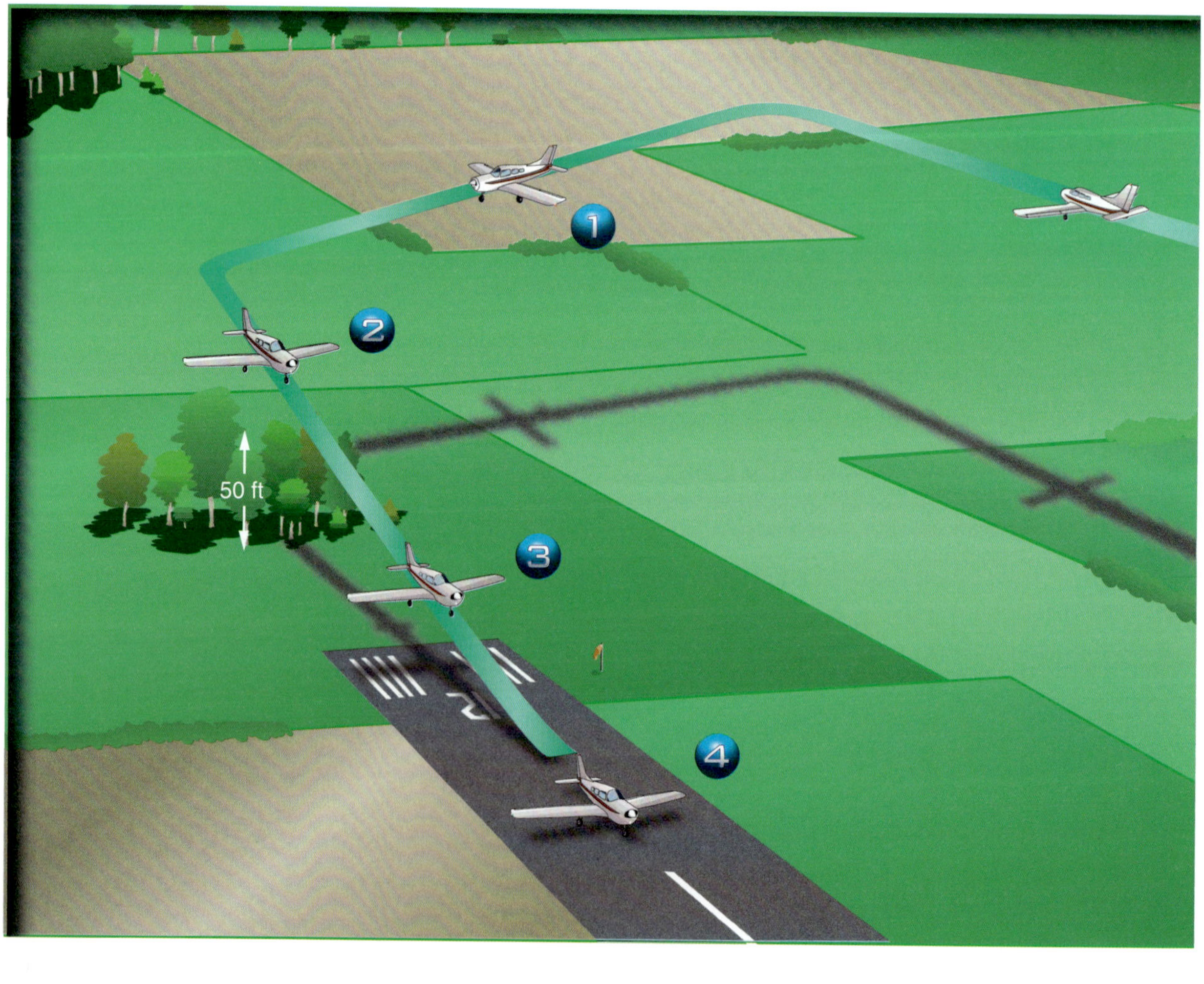

Short-Field Approach And Landing

The descent angle used for the short-field approach is steeper than that used for a normal approach. This allows you to clear an obstacle located near the approach end of the runway. Extending full flaps allows a steeper descent angle without an increase in airspeed, which results in a decrease in the distance required to bring the airplane to a full stop.

Landing

 As you begin the flare, reduce power smoothly to idle and allow the airplane to touch down in a full-stall condition. Since the short-field approach is made at a steep descent angle and close to the airplane's stalling speed, you must judge the initiation of the flare accurately to avoid flying into the ground or stalling prematurely and sinking rapidly.

Reducing power too rapidly may result in an immediate increase in the rate of descent and a hard landing. On the other hand, the airplane should touch down with little or no float. An excessive amount of airspeed may result in touchdown too far beyond the runway threshold and a roll-out which exceeds the available landing area. As your training progresses, your goal will be to touch down beyond and within 200 feet of a point specified by your instructor.

 When the airplane is firmly on the runway, lower the nose, retract the flaps (if recommended) and apply the brakes, as necessary to further shorten the roll-out.

Some manufacturers recommend retraction of flaps on the landing roll. This transfers more weight to the main gear and enhances braking.

SHORT-FIELD APPROACH AND LANDING

To meet the PTS requirements, you must:

- Exhibit knowledge of the elements related to a short-field approach and landing.
- Consider the wind conditions, landing surface, obstructions, and select the most suitable touchdown point.
- Establish the recommended approach and landing configuration and airspeed; adjust pitch attitude and power as required.
- Maintain a stabilized approach and recommended approach airspeed, or in its absence not more than 1.3 V_{SO}, +10/–5 knots, with wind gust factor applied.
- Make smooth, timely, and correct control application during the roundout and touchdown.
- Touch down smoothly at minimum control airspeed.
- Touch down at or within 200 feet (60 meters) beyond a specified point, with no side drift, minimum float and with the airplane's longitudinal axis aligned with and over the runway center/landing path.
- Maintain crosswind correction and directional control throughout the approach and landing sequence.
- Apply brakes as necessary, to stop in the shortest distance consistent with safety.
- Complete the appropriate checklist.

28 — SOFT-FIELD TAKEOFF AND CLIMB

A soft field may be defined as any runway that measurably retards acceleration during the takeoff roll. The objective of the soft-field takeoff is to transfer the weight of the airplane from the landing gear to the wings as quickly and smoothly as possible to eliminate the drag caused by surfaces such as tall grass, soft dirt, or snow. Takeoffs and climbs from soft fields require special procedures, as well as knowledge of your aircraft's performance characteristics including V_X and V_Y.

You actually begin the soft-field procedure during the taxi phase. If the taxi area surface is soft, use full back pressure on the yoke to maintain full-up elevator (or stabilator) deflection with a slight amount of power to keep the airplane moving. This technique transfers some of the airplane's weight from the nosewheel to the main wheels, resulting in lower power requirements and greater ease in taxiing.

 Complete the before takeoff check on a paved or firm surface area, if practical. This helps to avoid propeller damage and the possibility of the airplane becoming stuck.

- Set the flap position as recommended by the manufacturer.

- Clear the approach and departure areas and the traffic pattern prior to taxiing onto the runway. After obtaining a clearance (at a controlled airport) or self announcing your intentions (at an uncontrolled airport), taxi into position for takeoff without stopping.

 Align the airplane with the center of the runway and while still rolling, advance the throttle smoothly to takeoff power. Maintain full back pressure on the yoke to raise the nosewheel from the soft surface.

> When the nosewheel is clear of the runway, nosewheel steering becomes ineffective. However, due to the increasing air flow, the rudder becomes sufficient for maintaining directional control.

- As you increase speed and the elevator (or stabilator) becomes more effective, reduce back pressure slightly. Continue to use back pressure on the yoke to hold the nose up and to reduce the amount of weight on the nosewheel.

Short-Field Takeoff And Climb

If you do not release some back pressure while accelerating during the takeoff roll, the airplane may assume an extremely nose-high attitude, which can cause the tail skid to come in contact with the runway.

 3. As the airplane lifts from the runway surface, reduce back pressure to achieve a level flight attitude.

As the airspeed increases, lift increases and more of the aircraft's weight is transferred to the wings. This causes the airplane to become airborne at an airspeed slower than safe climb speed. The airplane is now flying in ground effect.

 4. Allow the airplane to accelerate in level flight, within ground effect, to V_X before starting a climb.

On a rough surface the airplane may skip or bounce into the air before its full weight can be supported aerodynamically. Therefore, it is important to hold the pitch attitude as constant as possible (an important application of slow flight). If you permit the nose to lower after a bounce, the nosewheel may strike the ground. On the other hand, sharply increasing the pitch attitude after a bounce may cause the airplane to stall.

 5. Once all obstacles are cleared (if applicable), accelerate to V_Y. Retract the landing gear (if applicable) and raise the flaps (if applicable) once you have attained a safe altitude and airspeed. Trim to relieve control pressures.

 **SOFT-FIELD TAKEOFF AND CLIMB**

To meet the PTS requirements, you must:

- Exhibit knowledge of the elements related to a soft-field takeoff and climb.
- Position the flight controls for existing wind conditions and to maximize lift as quickly as possible.
- Clear the area; taxi onto the takeoff surface at a speed consistent with safety without stopping while advancing the throttle smoothly to takeoff power.
- Establish and maintain a pitch attitude that will transfer the weight of the airplane from the wheels to the wings as rapidly as possible.
- Lift off at the lowest possible airspeed and remain in ground effect while accelerating to V_X or V_Y, as appropriate.
- Establish a pitch altitude for V_X or V_Y, as appropriate, and maintain selected airspeed +10/–5 knots, during the climb.
- Retract the landing gear, if appropriate, and flaps after clear of any obstacles or as recommended by the manufacturer.
- Maintain takeoff power to a safe maneuvering altitude.
- Maintain directional control and proper wind-drift correction throughout the takeoff and climb.
- Complete the appropriate checklist.

29 — Soft-Field Approach And Landing

The objective of a soft-field landing is to ease the weight of the airplane from the wings to the main landing gear as gently and slowly as possible while keeping the nosewheel off the soft surface during most of the landing roll. This technique will prevent the nosewheel from sinking into the soft surface and reduce the possibility of an abrupt stop during the landing roll. You should consult your airplane's POH for the appropriate speeds and specific procedures for performing soft-field landings. Since the same general procedures used to execute a normal approach and landing apply to this discussion, only the additional techniques required to perform a soft-field approach and landing are explained here.

Approach

 Ensure that the before landing checklist is completed and that the area is clear. Extend approximately one-third of the available flaps during the latter portion of the downwind leg and two-thirds on base, while progressively reducing the airspeed. Trim to relieve control pressures.

 Unless obstacles are in the approach path, maintain the same descent angle on final as you would during a normal approach. Maintain the recommended approach speed and extend the remaining flaps.

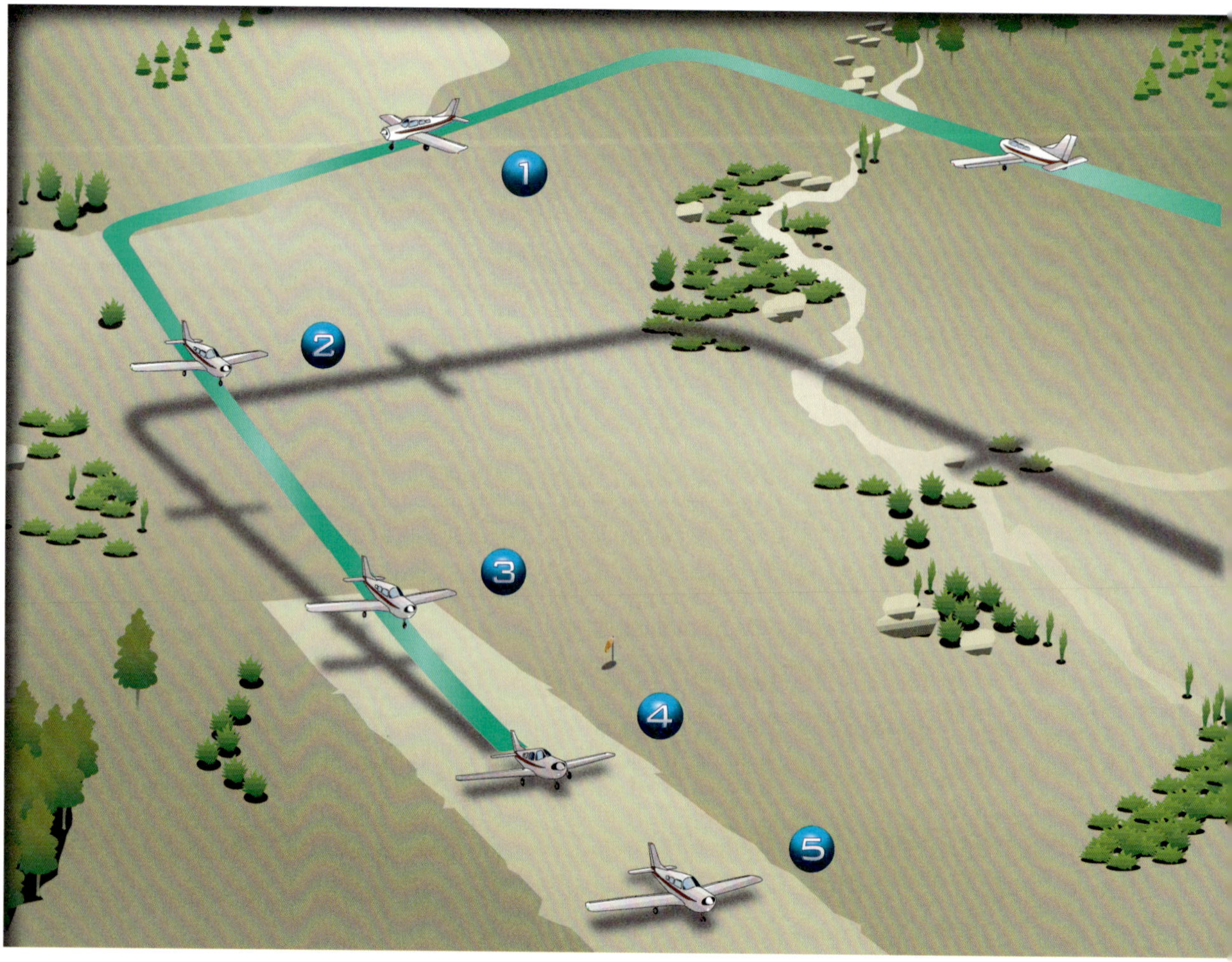

Short-Field Approach and Landing

The use of flaps during a soft-field landing is normally recommended to allow the airplane to touch down at a minimum speed. However, you must also consider the runway conditions when determining whether to use full flaps. For example, in a low-wing aircraft, the flaps may suffer damage from mud, slush, or stones thrown up from the wheels.

Landing

 Hold the airplane one to two feet above the surface as long as possible to dissipate forward speed. Maintain that attitude with power and slowly continue the descent until the airplane touches down at the lowest possible airspeed with the airplane in a nose-high attitude.

When you maintain power during the landing flare and touchdown, the slipstream flow over the empennage increases the effectiveness of the elevator (or stabilator). The amount of power required during the landing flare and touchdown varies with the weight and density altitude.

 After touchdown, maintain back pressure on the yoke to hold the nosewheel off the surface as long as practical. As the airspeed decreases on the roll-out, smoothly and gently lower the nosewheel to the surface.

Adding a small amount of power after touchdown will help you to ease the nosewheel down, under control.

 Increase the power slightly, if necessary, to keep the aircraft moving and prevent it from stopping suddenly on the soft surface. Avoid using the brakes since braking action may cause the nosewheel to dig into the soft surface and may damage the landing gear. The soft surface should provide sufficient braking action to slow the aircraft down.

SOFT-FIELD APPROACH AND LANDING

To meet the PTS requirements, you must:

- Exhibit knowledge of the elements related to a soft-field approach and landing.

- Consider the wind conditions, landing surface and obstructions, and select the most suitable touchdown area.

- Establish the recommended approach and landing configuration, and airspeed; adjust pitch attitude and power as required.

- Maintain a stablized approach and recommended airspeed, or in its absence not more than 1.3 V_{SO}, +10/–5 knots, with wind gust factor applied.

- Make smooth, timely, and correct control application during the roundout and touchdown.

- Touch down softly with no drift, and with the airplane's longitudinal axis aligned with the runway/landing path.

- Maintain crosswind correction and directional control thoughout the approach and landing sequence.

- Maintain proper position of the flight controls and sufficient speed to taxi on the soft surface.

- Complete the appropriate checklist.

EXERCISES — PERFORMANCE TAKEOFFS AND LANDINGS

26 — Short-Field Takeoff And Climb

1. Name two situations which require the use of a short-field takeoff and climb.

2. During short-field practice sessions, it is assumed that you must clear an obstacle which is how many feet in height? _____

3. True/False. You should use the best rate-of-climb speed to clear obstacles at the departure end of the runway. _____

4. Why should you hold the brakes until you achieve full power prior to beginning the takeoff roll?

5. Why should you avoid raising the nose prior to the recommended liftoff speed?

27 — Short-Field Approach And Landing

1. In what situations would executing a short-field approach and landing be necessary?

2. Is the descent angle for a short-field approach steeper, shallower, or the same as that flown for a normal approach to a landing? _____

3. What is the purpose of extending full flaps when executing a short-field approach?

4. True/False. While executing a short-field landing, you should reduce power to idle in the flare and allow the airplane to touch down in a full-stall condition. _____

5. What can occur if you maintain an excessive amount of airspeed during the short-field approach and landing?

EXERCISE — PERFORMANCE TAKEOFFS AND LANDINGS

28 — SOFT-FIELD TAKEOFF AND CLIMB

1. What is the objective of a soft-field takeoff?

2. What is the definition of a soft field?

3. True/False. The soft-field procedure begins during the taxi phase. _____

4. What can occur if you do not release some back pressure while accelerating during the takeoff roll?

5. Since liftoff normally occurs at a speed below the safe climb speed, what action should you take before starting a climb?

29 — SOFT-FIELD APPROACH AND LANDING

1. What is the objective of a soft-field landing?

2. Why is the extension of flaps normally recommended for a soft-field approach and landing?

3. When executing a soft-field landing, why should you hold the airplane one to two feet above the runway as long as possible?

4. True/False. During a soft-field landing, you should lower the nosewheel to the surface as quickly as possible after touchdown. _____

5. What is the correct procedure for the roll-out after a soft-field landing? _____
   A. Maintain power at idle and apply heavy braking.
   B. Hold forward pressure on the yoke and avoid braking.
   C. Maintain back pressure on the yoke and increase power slightly, if necessary.

SPECIAL FLIGHT OPERATIONS

SPECIAL FLIGHT OPERATIONS

SPECIAL FLIGHT OPERATIONS

MANEUVER 30 8-2
   ATTITUDE INSTRUMENT FLYING

MANEUVER 31 8-10
   NIGHT OPERATIONS

EXERCISES 8-15

Video Volume II — Flight Maneuvers, Ground Reference Maneuvers, Performance Takeoffs and Landings, and Special Flight Operations

30 — Attitude Instrument Flying

Attitude instrument flying is a fundamental method for controlling an airplane by reference to instruments. Basic instrument maneuver training is not intended to prepare you for unrestricted flight into instrument meteorological conditions (IMC). Rather, it is an emergency procedure to prepare you for an inadvertent incursion into IMC. For example, if you inadvertently enter an overcast layer of clouds, the procedure calls for a 180° standard-rate turn to fly out of IMC. During your training, you will develop a good understanding of the flight instruments and systems which will help you build the skills required to interpret and translate the information presented into precise airplane control. One such skill is the instrument scan, which is a methodical cross-check of the flight instruments. Your scan should resemble a wagon wheel with the attitude indicator as the hub and the spokes extending out to the other instruments. A typical scan might progress as follows: attitude indicator, altimeter, attitude indicator, VSI, attitude indicator, heading indicator, attitude indicator, turn coordinator, attitude indicator, airspeed indicator, attitude indicator, and so on. At first, you may have a tendency to scan rapidly, looking directly at the instruments without knowing exactly what information you are seeking. However, with familiarity and practice, the instrument scan reveals definite trends during specific flight conditions. These trends will help you control the airplane as it makes a transition from one flight condition to another.

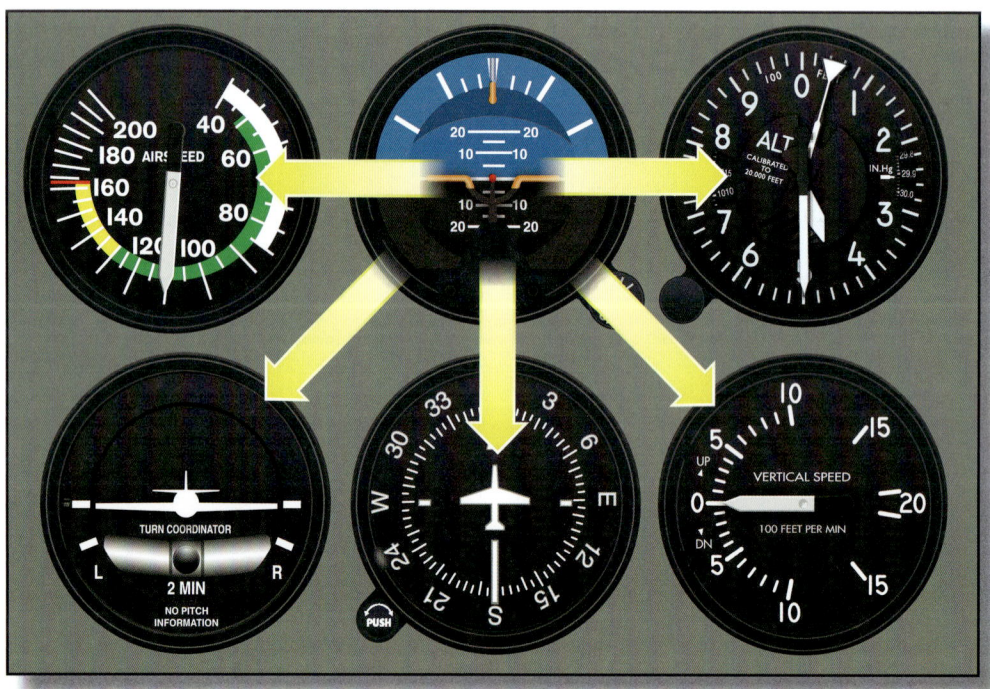

If you apply your full concentration to a single instrument, you will encounter a problem called fixation. This results from a natural human inclination to observe a specific instrument carefully and accurately, often to the exclusion of other instruments. Fixation on a single instrument usually results in poor control. For example, while performing a turn, you may have a tendency to watch only the turn coordinator instead of including other instruments in your cross-check. This fixation on the turn coordinator may lead to a loss of altitude through poor pitch and bank control. You should look at each instrument only long enough to understand the information it presents, then continue on to the next one. Similarly, you may find yourself placing too much emphasis on a single instrument, instead of relying on a combination of instruments necessary for airplane performance information. This differs from fixation in that you are using other instruments, but are giving too much attention to a particular one.

Attitude Instrument Flying

During performance of a maneuver, you may sometimes fail to anticipate significant instrument indications following attitude changes. For example, during leveloff from a climb or descent, you may concentrate on pitch control, while forgetting about heading or roll information. This error, called omission, results in erratic control of heading and bank.

To fly effectively by instrument reference, you should understand each instrument's operating principles and limitations. In addition, you need to know what each instrument reveals about the airplane's performance. Each flight maneuver involves the use of combinations of instruments that you must read and interpret in order to control the airplane. For example, if you want to control pitch attitude, primarily use the attitude indicator, airspeed indicator, altimeter, and vertical speed indicator. To control bank attitude, primarily use the attitude indicator, turn coordinator, and heading indicator. To control an airplane by reference to instruments, you must continue perfecting the techniques of proper pitch, bank, and power control that you practiced during flight by visual reference. Maintain a light touch on the controls and trim to relieve any control pressures once the airplane has stabilized in a particular attitude.

Basic attitude instrument training provides you with the foundation for further instrument training which could lead to the addition of an instrument rating. Specific instrument maneuvers which you will perform during your private pilot training include straight-and-level flight, constant airspeed climbs and descents, turns to headings, and recovery from unusual flight attitudes. When flying with a view limiting device such as a hood or JeppShades, your flight instructor will act as safety pilot; never practice attitude instrument flight solo.

STRAIGHT-AND-LEVEL

Straight-and-level flight is the starting point and building block for all attitude instrument flying. You will be challenged by your flight instructor to develop your instrument scanning technique and the skills required to accurately control the airplane.

1. With your view limiting device in place, set the power for normal cruise flight.

2. Adjust the pitch attitude for level flight by positioning the miniature airplane on the horizon bar of the attitude indicator. Hold the pitch attitude and trim to relieve control pressures. Maintain the proper pitch attitude using the attitude indicator, altimeter, VSI, and the airspeed indicator.

   - The attitude indicator is the only instrument which provides a pictorial display of the airplane's overall attitude. During instrument flight, all changes in pitch and bank are made by reference to this instrument. The other instruments are used to indicate when a change in attitude is required.

> When adjusting pitch using the attitude indicator, you should initially restrict the displacement of the horizon bar to a one-half bar width up or down, progressing later to a full bar width. Use greater displacement only when large attitude changes are required.

   - The altimeter provides an indication of pitch attitude. At a constant airspeed and power setting, altitude is controlled by pitch. Since the altitude should remain constant when the airplane is in level flight, any deviation from the desired altitude indicates the need for a pitch change. Obviously, if the altitude is increasing, the nose must be lowered. The rate of movement of the altimeter needle is as important as its direction of movement in maintaining level flight. Large pitch attitude deviations from level flight result in rapid altitude changes; slight pitch deviations produce much slower changes in the altimeter needle movement. Remember to make all adjustments to pitch by using the attitude indicator.

> If the deviation from the desired altitude is less than 100 feet, you can make the attitude adjustment you need to return to the correct altitude without changing the power setting. However, if the deviation from the desired altitude is greater than 100 feet, you should make a change in power setting and an appropriate trim adjustment.

ATTITUDE INSTRUMENT FLYING

- Normally, the vertical speed indicator's function is to help you establish and maintain a desired rate of climb or descent. Due to the design of the instrument, there is a lag of approximately six to nine seconds before the correct rate of change is registered. Even though this lag exists, you may use the vertical speed indicator as a trend instrument for maintaining a desired pitch attitude. As a trend instrument, it indicates the direction of pitch change almost instantaneously. If the needle deviates from the zero position, the instrument is indicating that the pitch is changing. Apply corrective pressures while referring to the attitude indicator. This pressure will stop the needle movement and place the airplane in a level attitude again. However, you should not try to return the needle to zero, since the lag in the vertical speed indicator will cause a tendency to overcontrol.

As a guide, adjust the miniature airplane on the attitude indicator to produce a rate of change which is double the amount of altitude deviation, and use power as necessary. For example, if an airplane is 100 feet below the desired altitude, select a climb rate of 200 f.p.m. Estimate the initial amount of pitch change required to stop the descent and climb at 200 f.p.m. Hold the pitch constant until the vertical speed indicator displays an accurate rate, then adjust it as necessary.

- The airspeed indicator also indicates pitch attitude. If you establish a constant pitch attitude and power setting and permit the airplane to stabilize, the airspeed remains constant. As you raise the pitch attitude, the airspeed decreases slightly. On the other hand, as you lower the pitch attitude, the airspeed increases somewhat. A rapid change in airspeed indicates that a large pitch change has occurred; you should apply smooth control pressure in the opposite direction. Again, however, look at the attitude indicator to note the amount of pitch change caused by control pressure. This will help you avoid overcontrolling the airplane. You will know the airplane is passing through approximately level flight when the needle stops its movement in one direction and begins to move in the opposite direction.

3. Confirm wings level on the attitude indicator. Maintain your bank attitude using the attitude indicator, heading indicator, and turn coordinator.

    - The principal instrument used for bank control is the attitude indicator. The heading indicator and turn coordinator are used to indicate when a change in bank is required.

    - In coordinated flight, bank attitude also is indicated on the heading indicator. Generally, if the heading displayed on the indicator is not changing, the wings are level. On the other hand, a slow heading change indicates a shallow bank angle, while a rapid change in heading indicates a steep bank.

To make a heading change, use a bank angle equal to one-half of the difference between the present heading and the desired heading. However, the angle you use should not exceed that necessary for a standard-rate turn. For example, if your desired heading is 300° and your present heading is 290°, you need to change your heading by 10°. Therefore, you should use a bank angle no greater than one-half of 10° or, in this example, 5° of bank.

- When the miniature airplane of the turn coordinator is in a wings-level position, the airplane is maintaining a constant heading. If the wings of the miniature airplane are displaced from the level flight position, the airplane is turning in the direction that the miniature airplane is banking. Remember that the ball in the inclinometer indicates whether you are maintaining coordinated flight. If the ball is off center, the airplane is slipping or skidding. When this occurs, make corrections with appropriate coordinated rudder and aileron pressure.

STRAIGHT-AND-LEVEL FLIGHT

To meet the PTS requirements, you must:

- Exhibit knowledge of the elements related to attitude instrument flying during straight-and-level flight.
- Maintain straight-and-level flight solely by reference to instruments using proper instrument cross-check and interpretation, and coordinated control application.
- Maintain altitude, ±200 feet (60 meters); heading, ±20 degrees; and airspeed, ±10 knots.

CONSTANT AIRSPEED CLIMBS

This basic maneuver will help you improve your scan, maintain a heading, and climb to a specific altitude. In a constant airspeed climb you should include the attitude indicator, airspeed indicator, vertical speed indicator, and altimeter in your scan for pitch information. Refer to the heading indicator and turn coordinator for bank and heading information.

1. From straight-and-level cruise flight, initiate a wings-level climb by positioning the miniature airplane to an approximate nose-high indication (about two bar widths). Simultaneously, add power to maintain the desired climb speed. Apply right rudder as necessary to counteract the effect of P-factor. Maintain directional control by referring to the attitude indicator, heading indicator, and turn coordinator.

2. Once the climb is stabilized, trim to relieve control pressures. Continue scanning and make any required corrections by referring to the attitude indicator.

3. Approximately 50 feet prior to reaching your desired altitude, begin the leveloff by applying forward pressure on the yoke to adjust the miniature airplane down to the horizon of the attitude indicator.

> Use approximately 10% of the climb rate as a rule of thumb to determine when to begin your leveloff. For example, if your climb rate is 500 f.p.m., begin your leveloff roughly 50 feet before the desired altitude.

4. As the airplane accelerates, use less right rudder pressure. Trim to relieve control pressures.

5. As you reach cruise speed, reduce power to the recommended cruise setting and trim for straight-and-level flight.

CONSTANT AIRSPEED CLIMBS

To meet the PTS requirements, you must:

- Exhibit knowledge of the elements related to attitude instrument flying during constant airspeed climbs.
- Establish the climb configuration specified by the examiner.
- Transition to the climb pitch attitude and power setting on an assigned heading using proper instrument cross-check and interpretation, and coordinated control application.
- Demonstrate climbs solely by reference to instruments at a constant airspeed to specific altitudes in straight flight and turns.
- Level off at the assigned altitude and maintain that altitude, ±200 feet (60 meters); maintain heading, ±20 degrees; maintain airspeed, ±10 knots.

ATTITUDE INSTRUMENT FLYING

CONSTANT AIRSPEED DESCENTS

This maneuver will help you improve your scan, maintain a heading, and descend to a specific altitude. In a constant airspeed descent you should include the attitude indicator, airspeed indicator, vertical speed indicator, and altimeter in your scan for pitch information and the heading indicator and turn coordinator for bank and heading information.

1. From straight-and-level flight, apply carburetor heat (if applicable) and simultaneously decrease power while gradually increasing back pressure on the yoke to maintain altitude and slow down.

2. Once the desired airspeed is attained, further reduce the power (if necessary) and simultaneously lower the nose to maintain the desired airspeed. Trim to relieve control pressures.

3. Maintain a constant airspeed during the descent. Correct for airspeed deviations by adjusting pitch attitude, not power. You can obtain pitch information by cross-checking the airspeed indicator, attitude indicator, altimeter, and VSI.

4. Approximately 50 feet prior to your desired attitude, begin the level off by simultaneously adding power and raising the nose to place the miniature airplane of the attitude indicator on the horizon bar.

Use the 10% rule of thumb to determine when to begin your leveloff. For example, if your descent rate is 500 f.p.m., begin your leveloff roughly 50 feet before the desired altitude.

5. Once the pitch attitude and airspeed have stabilized in straight-and-level flight, trim to relieve control pressures.

 CONSTANT AIRSPEED DESCENTS

To meet the PTS requirements, you must:

- Exhibit knowledge of the elements related to attitude instrument flying during constant airspeed descents.
- Establish the descent configuration specified by the examiner.
- Transition to the descent pitch attitude and power setting on an assigned heading using proper instrument cross-check and interpretation, and coordinated control application.
- Demonstrate descents solely by reference to instruments at a constant airspeed to specific altitudes in straight flight and turns.
- Level off at the assigned altitude and maintain that altitude, ±200 feet (60 meters); maintain heading, ±20 degrees; maintain airspeed, ±10 knots.

TURNS TO HEADINGS

To further develop your attitude instrument flying skills your will practice level turns to specific headings. To maintain the desired altitude during the turns you will have to closely coordinate your pitch and power adjustments.

1. From straight-and-level flight, simultaneously apply coordinated aileron and rudder pressure in the direction of the turn. Use the attitude indicator to establish the approximate angle of bank required for a standard rate turn.

A rule of thumb to determine the approximate angle of bank required for a standard rate turn is to divide your airspeed by 10 and add one-half the result. For example, 120 ÷ 10 = 12, 12 + 6 = 18, so 18° is the approximate angle of bank required for a standard rate turn at 120 knots. At 80 knots, a standard rate turn would require about a 12° angle of bank.

2. As you establish the turn, adjust the nose of the miniature airplane so that it is slightly above the level flight position on the horizon bar. Add power if necessary to maintain airspeed. Trim to relieve control pressures.

3. Once you are established in a standard rate turn, neutralize the aileron and rudder inputs. Check the turn coordinator to determine if you are maintaining a standard rate turn. Make any corrections using the attitude indicator. Cross-check the altimeter to ensure you are maintaining a constant altitude. Also, include the heading indicator in your scan to determine your progress toward the desired heading.

4. To roll out of the turn, apply coordinated aileron and rudder pressure opposite the direction of turn. Also, apply forward pressure on the yoke to prevent a gain in altitude. Simultaneously, reduce power to maintain airspeed. Use the attitude indicator as the principal reference instrument during the roll-out.

A guideline to determine the amount of lead for the roll-out from the turn is approximately 1/2 the angle of bank. For example, if you held 18° of bank for your turn, you should begin your roll-out about 9° before the desired heading.

5. Once you return to straight-and-level flight, continue your instrument scan and trim to relieve control pressures.

TURNS TO HEADINGS

To meet the PTS requirements, you must be able to:

- Exhibits knowledge of the elements related to attitude instrument flying during turns to headings.

- Transitions to the level-turn attitude using proper instrument cross-check and interpretation, and coordinated control application.

- Demonstrates turns to headings solely by reference to instruments; maintains altitude, ± 200 feet (60 meters); maintains a standard rate turn and rolls out on the assigned heading, ± 10 degrees; maintains airspeed, ± 10 knots.

RECOVERY FROM UNUSUAL FLIGHT ATTITUDES

Unusual flight attitudes can be a result of many factors such as turbulence, confusion, preoccupation with cabin duties, carelessness, or a lack of proficiency in basic airplane control. Regardless of the cause of an unusual flight attitude, it usually is unintentional and unexpected. There are two basic scenarios you will practice during your flight training — a nose-high attitude with rapidly decreasing airspeed, and a nose-low attitude with a rapidly increasing airspeed. Learning to recognize and promptly recover from an unusual attitude is a key part of attitude instrument training. Before initiating any recovery, quickly confirm the indications on the attitude indicator are correct by scanning the other instruments.

NOSE-HIGH ATTITUDE

You will recognize a nose-high attitude by the indication of the miniature airplane on the attitude indicator, as well as a rapidly increasing altimeter, positive rate of climb, and a rapidly decreasing airspeed. Since a rapid decrease in airspeed can quickly result in a stall, prompt recognition and recovery form a nose-high unusual attitude is essential.

1. Simultaneously, lower the nose to place the miniature airplane on the horizon bar of the attitude indicator and add power (if available) to prevent a loss of airspeed.

2. If the airplane is in a bank, level the wings.

3. After you return to straight-and-level flight and airspeed returns to normal, reduce power to a cruise setting and trim to relieve control pressures.

Nose-Low Attitude

Like a nose-high attitude, a nose-low attitude can be recognized on the attitude indicator by the position of the miniature airplane. You can confirm a nose-low attitude by a rapidly decreasing altitude, a high rate of descent, and a rapidly increasing airspeed. Airspeed is again a critical element. However, in this case, your airspeed can quickly exceed maneuvering speed with a potential for overstressing the airplane during the recovery.

1. Simultaneously, reduce power and level the wings using coordinated aileron and rudder pressure and referencing the miniature airplane of the attitude indicator.

2. Raise the nose of the airplane to a level flight attitude.

If you attempt to raise the nose before you roll wings level, the increased load factor can result in accelerated stall, a spin, or a force exceeding the airplane's design limits.

3. After you return the airplane to straight-and-level flight and airspeed returns to normal, add power to a cruise setting and trim to relieve control pressures.

RECOVERY FROM UNUSUAL FLIGHT ATTITUDES

To meet the PTS requirements, you must:

- Exhibit knowledge of the elements related to attitude instrument flying during unusual attitudes.

- Recognize unusual flight attitudes solely by reference to instruments; recover promptly to a stabilized level flight attitude using proper instrument cross-check and interpretation and smooth, coordinated control application in the correct sequence.

31 — Night Operations

In many respects, night flying is more pleasant than daytime flying. At night, the air is generally smoother and cooler which results in a more comfortable flight and better airplane performance. In addition, at night you normally experience less airport traffic and less competition when using communication frequencies. Although night flying can be enjoyable for you and your passengers, there are special considerations you should take into account, particularly with regard to preflight preparation, airport operations, night navigation, and night emergencies. A good understanding of the limitations of night vision and night visual illusions is particularly important. For more information about night flying and the associated physiological aspects, you can refer to Chapter 10, Section A, of the *Private Pilot Manual*.

Preflight

Preparation for a night flight is inherently more detailed than for a daytime flight. For example, the preflight inspection for a daytime flight normally would not include the landing, taxi, position, and cockpit lights. When performing your preflight inspection at night, pay very close attention to the details of the checklist, and, if possible, conduct the preflight inspection in a well-lighted area. At some airports, the ramps are not lighted; therefore, it may be preferable to plan for an earlier departure so you can complete your preflight inspection before dark.

Your airplane may have fuses which are accessible to you during flight. If this is the case you must ensure a spare set is available in the airplane. If the airplane is equipped with circuit breakers, check to see that they are not tripped. Since most circuit breakers can not be tripped manually, one that is tripped may be an indication of an equipment malfunction. To check a tripped circuit breaker, simply reset it and then check the associated equipment for proper operation.

Exterior Lighting

During your preflight inspection, you should check the lighting systems such as the position lights located on the tail and wing tips; however, turn them on only long enough to verify proper operation, then turn each system off to conserve the airplane battery. Some airplanes have small plastic attachments on the wing tips which reflect light so you can check the operation of the position lights from the cockpit. Additionally, your airplane must be equipped with an anticollision light system which must be checked and operational for night flying.

Most airplanes have landing lights, and some have taxi lights, which must be checked for operation during your preflight. These lights may be collocated behind a common lens in the engine cowling or in the leading edge of the wing. Many high performance airplanes have the landing and taxi lights mounted on the landing gear. Your preflight check should include inspection for proper illumination, condition of the lens, and the correct alignment of each light. When operating the landing and taxi lights, avoid shining them in the direction of another aircraft, since this can impair the other pilot's night vision. Even though landing and taxi lights generally are not required for night flying, when they are installed they should be checked for proper operation.

NIGHT OPERATIONS

INTERIOR LIGHTING

Another important part of your preflight inspection is a check of the cabin and instrument panel lighting systems. The instruments and instrument panel may be lighted in one of several ways. The first is commonly referred to as flood lighting, the second is post lighting, and the third method of instrument illumination is internal, with each instrument containing a light within the case. Flood lighting is probably the most common for training type airplanes. This system uses a single centrally-mounted light with a rheostat to regulate the intensity. Post lighting provides a light source adjacent to each instrument. Each light is directed toward the instruments and is shaded from your vision. This system may incorporate two or more rheostats — one for the flight instruments, and another for the engine instruments. In addition, there may be other controls for illumination of fuel tank selectors, switch panels, radios, and convenience lighting. Internal instrument lighting is similar to post lighting, except that the light source is located inside the instrument itself. The magnetic compass and the radios are good examples of internal lighting. Luminescent lettering is often used with internal lighting to enhance clarity.

Before any night flight you should become thoroughly familiar with the airplane's cabin, instrumentation, and control layout. Since some switches and circuit breaker panels may be hard to see at night, be sure that you are able to locate them in poor light conditions. Make sure you have at least one reliable flashlight. This should be standard equipment for any night flight. Finally, organize and place your flashlight, plotter, aviation computer, charts, pencil, and other necessities in a location that is easily accessible.

ENGINE START, TAXI, AND RUNUP

Due to limited visibility and illusions created by low light conditions, night airport operations can be very different than those you are accustomed to during daytime. At night it is difficult for other persons to determine that you intend to start the engine. Therefore, in addition to calling out "CLEAR," momentarily turn on the anticollision light, the position lights, or other airplane lights to warn others that the propeller is about to rotate.

Wait until you are actually ready to taxi before you turn on the taxi light. Since taxi and landing lights usually cast a beam which is narrow and concentrated, illumination to the side of the airplane is minimal and taxi speed should be slower at night, especially in congested ramp areas. Once in the runup area, turn the taxi and landing lights off until your runup is complete. While you can usually detect any unintended forward movement of the airplane during the day, the airplane may creep forward at night without you noticing. Therefore, it is important that you maintain constant brake pressure throughout your runup and stay alert for any unintentional movement.

TAKEOFF AND CLIMB

During the takeoff roll, select a reference point down the runway, such as the point where the runway edge lights seem to converge. As you liftoff, you may notice a lack of reliable outside visual references. This is particularly true at small airports located in sparsely populated areas. To compensate for this effect, maintain your orientation using the flight instruments in conjunction with available outside visual references. During your initial climbout, maintain a normal climb attitude on the attitude indicator. Then, cross-check the vertical speed indicator, altimeter, and the airspeed indicator. The first 500 feet of altitude gain after takeoff is considered to be a critical period since you are transitioning from the comparatively well-lighted airport area into what sometimes appears as total darkness.

NAVIGATION

Navigation at night is usually fairly simple because the outlines of major cities and towns are clearly discernible. With sufficient altitude, major metropolitan areas are visible during favorable weather from distances up to 100 miles or more. Major highways tend to stand out at night because of the presence of numerous automobile headlights. Less traveled roads are usually not so easy to see,

Night Operations

unless the moonlight is bright enough to illuminate them. On clear, moonlit nights, outlines of the terrain and other surface features are dimly visible. For example, you can often discern the outlines of bodies of water by noting the reflection of the moonlight. However, on extremely dark nights, terrain features are nearly invisible, except in brightly lighted, populated areas.

A subdued white cabin light is recommended for reading charts. If a map reading light is not available in the airplane, use your flashlight for reading the charts. Remember, white light adversely affects your night vision, so the intensity of the light should be kept to the minimum.

Due to the reduction in outside visual references, you may have a tendency to spend too much time looking at the flight instruments. Therefore, you must make a special effort to devote enough time to scan for traffic. You also should make sure the scan pattern you develop covers all the sky you can see from the cockpit, both horizontally and vertically. However, keep in mind that the off-center viewing technique is recommended at night. While scanning, look for position light relationships of other aircraft to help determine their direction of flight.

LANDING

Many pilots have a tendency to make higher or lower approaches at night than during the daytime. Therefore, give careful consideration to traffic pattern procedures and to the factors that enable you to maintain the proper descent angle on final approach. Visual glideslope indicators, if available, provide an excellent visual cue for descent angle guidance. Fly a normal approach pattern using the altimeter and vertical speed indicator to monitor the rate of descent. As you near the runway, the runway lights provide an effective peripheral vision cue for beginning the landing flare. When viewed with your peripheral vision, runway lights seem to rise and spread laterally as you near the touchdown point.

It is standard operating procedure to use your landing lights for night landings, even though they may cause an illusion of runway height. The portion of the runway illuminated by the landing lights seems higher than the surrounding area, potentially leading to a high flare. In addition, focusing your attention on the area immediately in front of the airplane is poor practice even though the arrangement of most landing lights tends to encourage this technique. When using landing lights, your sighting point should be near the forward limit of the lighted area.

While you will make most of your night landings using landing lights, you should also practice landings without the aid of the landing lights. During no-light landings, you should begin your flare when the runway lights at the far end of the runway first appear to be rising higher than the airplane. This technique demands a smooth and timely flare using power and pitch changes as necessary for the airplane to settle softly on the runway.

NIGHT EMERGENCIES

When flying at night, especially during a night cross-country, high cruising altitudes provide an improved margin of safety. There are several reasons for this. First, range is usually greater at higher altitudes. Second, a higher altitude keeps you well above normal obstructions, and third, gliding distance is greater in the event of engine failure. For example, at 10,000 feet AGL, a light airplane with a glide ratio of 8 to 1 may glide 13 miles. This distance may place the airplane within range of an airport.

ENGINE FAILURE

Probably the most feared night emergency is an engine failure. If you should find yourself in a situation where a emergency landing at night is required, your first priority is to fly the airplane, maintain control, and use the same procedures as those recommended for daytime emergency landings. The landing light, if available, may be used during the final approach to assist you in avoiding obstacles in the approach path. Highways may be used as emergency landing strips at night, but you must exercise extreme caution to avoid power lines and vehicular traffic.

Inadvertent Entry Into IMC

A major safety concern for non-instrument rated pilots flying at night is unintentional flight into instrument meteorological conditions (IMC). It is easy to fly into an overcast condition at night because it is difficult to visually detect the clouds. Before you fly at night, obtain a thorough weather briefing. Give special attention to any information in the weather briefing that indicates possible formation of clouds, fog, or precipitation.

There are several guidelines that may help you avoid inadvertently entering IMC at night. If you are approaching an overcast, you can sometimes detect the presence of clouds when the lights in the distance disappear. In addition, a luminous glow, or halo, around the position lights indicates imminent or actual penetration of IMC. If you turn on the landing light, you will notice some scattering of the beam if there is considerable haze or if the temperature and dewpoint are converging rapidly and cloud formation is imminent. If you inadvertently enter a cloud layer, strobe type anticollision lights can be affected in the same way but the intensity of the light is much greater, possibly impairing your night vision. If you do penetrate IMC, calmly, but immediately, reference your flight instruments to initiate a 180° standard-rate turn to fly out of the weather conditions.

NIGHT PREPARATION

To meet the PTS requirements, you must demonstrate knowledge of:

- Physiological aspects of night flying as they relate to vision.

- Lighting systems identifying airports, runways, taxiways and obstructions, and pilot controlled lighting.

- Airplane lighting systems.

- Personal equipment essential for night flight.

- Night orientation, navigation, and chart reading techniques.

- Safety precautions and emergencies unique to night flying.

EXERCISES — SPECIAL FLIGHT OPERATIONS
30 — Attitude Instrument Flying

1. What instrument replaces the natural horizon during instrument flight?

2. True/False. The attitude indicator provides all the necessary information for flight during instrument conditions. _____

3. True/False. A tight grip on the yoke ensures smooth and precise attitude control. _____

4. During a constant airspeed climb, what action should you take to counteract the effect of P-factor?

5. During a constant airspeed descent, how should you correct for airspeed deviations?

6. Typically, at what altitude would you begin your level-off if your target altitude is 2,000 feet, and your rate of descent is 500 feet per minute? _____

7. What is the approximate angle of bank which will result in a standard rate turn for an airspeed of 100 knots? _____

8. What instrument should be referenced to confirm and maintain a standard rate turn?

9. What is the first step in recovering from a nose-high unusual attitude.

10. When recovering from a nose-low unusual attitude, why is it recommended that you level the wings before applying back pressure on the yoke?

EXERCISES — SPECIAL FLIGHT OPERATIONS

31 — NIGHT OPERATIONS

1. True/False. When checking the airplane lighting system you normally should leave the lights on only long enough to check for proper operation. _____

2. In addition to calling out "*CLEAR*," what other precaution can you take when starting the airplane's engine at night?

3. Why is it important to taxi slower at night than during the day?

4. How can you compensate for diminished outside visual reference during a night takeoff and climbout?

5. During a night flight, what should you do if you inadvertently fly into instrument meteorological conditions (IMC)?

ANSWERS — GROUND OPERATIONS

1 — Preflight Inspection

1. Use the appropriate checklist for your airplane

2. **A**irworthiness certificate; **R**egistration certificate; **R**adio station class license (if applicable); **O**perating instructions, POH, or approved flight manual; **W**eight and balance data, including equipment list

3. Water settles to the bottom of the tester since it is heavier than fuel.

4. True

5. B

2 — Engine Starting

1. False

2. The engine cylinders

3. Pilot's operating handbook (POH)

4. 60 seconds

5. Immediately shut down the engine to prevent possible damage.

3 — Taxiing

1. False

2. Decrease

3. Apply the brakes in the direction of the turn.

4. Fully turn the yoke to the left, placing the left aileron in the up position. Hold the yoke to maintain a neutral elevator position.

5. Fully turn the yoke to the left, placing the left aileron in the up position. Hold the yoke full forward to maintain the elevator (or stabilator) in the full down position.

4 — Before Takeoff Check

1. To improve engine cooling.

2. True

3. Decrease

4. Unreliable gyro indications

5. False

5 — Postflight Procedures

1. To prevent unfiltered air from being drawn into the carburetor.
2. Tune 121.5 MHz on a communication radio.
3. False
4. At the rib locations
5. In front of and behind the main wheels

BASIC MANEUVERS

6 — Straight-And-Level Flight

1. The natural horizon to the front and sides of your aircraft.
2. It helps you see and avoid other aircraft.
3. True
4. C
5. Cross-check the flight instruments

7 — Climbs

1. Best angle-of-climb speed
2. Best rate-of-climb speed
3. False
4. Decrease
5. 10%

8 — Descents

1. True
2. Higher
3. 4,050 feet MSL
4. False
5. Raise the nose

9 — Turns

1. Shallow: less than 20°; medium: 20° to 45°; steep: 45° or more
2. False
3. How long you deflect the ailerons
4. 075°
5. Add power

Answers

AIRPORT OPERATIONS

10 — Normal Takeoff And Climb

1. Close the throttle to abort the takeoff.

2. Apply right rudder.

3. Keep your hand on the throttle throughout the takeoff to ensure that it does not slide back during the takeoff roll and to enable you to close the throttle quickly if you decide to abort the takeoff.

4. The airplane may be forced into the air prematurely and then settle back to the runway. Also, the airplane may be at such a high angle of attack that it cannot accelerate to climb speed.

5. The standard procedure for departing an uncontrolled airport is to fly straight out or to make a 45° turn in the direction of the traffic pattern.

11 — Crosswind Takeoff And Climb

1. Refer to your airplane's POH.

2. False

3. Decrease

4. The airplane tracks straight down the runway and you feel no side load on the landing gear.

5. Enter a crab by making a coordinated turn into the wind.

12 — Traffic Patterns

1. Downwind, base, final, departure, and crosswind

2. True

3. 10 miles

4. 500 feet

5. "Front Range traffic, Piper 9163 Kilo, final, Runway 26, touch-and-go, Front Range."

13 — Normal Approach And Landing

1. False

2. The 180° position (position abeam the intended landing area)

3. Reduce power, extend flaps, or both.

4. Add power and decrease the pitch attitude slightly.

5. Flare, touchdown, and roll-out

6. Your heels should be on the floor so there is no tendency to use the brakes inadvertently.

Answers

7. Flying the airplane onto the runway with excess airspeed

8. A forward slip is used to steepen the airplane's descent angle to dissipate altitude without increasing the airspeed.

9. False

10. Add power immediately.

14 — Crosswind Approach and Landing

1. Crab method; wing-low (sidelip) method

2. Start your turn to final sooner and/or use up to 30° of bank.

3. C

4. Execute a go-around and land on a runway with more favorable wind conditions.

5. Increase

EMERGENCY LANDING PROCEDURES

15 — Systems and Equipment Malfunctions

1. Follow the checklist procedures specified in the POH and declare an emergency on the radio.

2. You may be able to continue flight to a suitable airport if you can maintain altitude or climb; otherwise, you must prepare for a forced landing and declare an emergency.

3. Maintain control of the airplane, then land as soon as practical and secure the door.

4. Immediately return the flaps control to the up, or previous position.

5. A dangerous situation can result if an asymmetrical flap extension occurs, resulting in loss of control at low altitude.

16 — Emergency Descent

1. True

2. False

3. 3,100 feet MSL

4. Never-exceed speed (V_{NE})

5. Maneuvering speed (V_A)

17 — Emergency Approach and Landing

1. Maintain control of the airplane and adjust the pitch to achieve best glide speed

2. When selecting a field, you must consider the wind direction and speed, length of the field, obstructions, and surface condition

Answers

3. False

4. 7700

5. Lowering the flaps shortens the glide distance.

FLIGHT MANEUVERS

18 — Slow Flight

1. An airspeed at which any further increase in angle of attack, increase in load factor, or reduction in power, would result in an immediate stall

2. 1,500 feet AGL

3. True

4. In increments

5. Altitude ± 100 feet; heading ± 10°, airspeed +10/-5 knots

19 — Power-Off Stalls

1. Landing configuration

2. 5 to 10 knots before the stall

3. Sudden loss of lift; nose dropping below the horizon; a rapid rate of descent

4. Raising the nose too quickly during stall recovery

5. False

20 — Power-On Stalls

1. During takeoffs and departure climbs

2. In the takeoff configuration

3. False

4. Decrease

5. 20°

21 — Demonstrated Stalls

1. False

2. False

3. False

4. Excessive back pressure stall

5. During a poorly planned and executed base turn to final approach and is often the result of overshooting the center of the runway during the turn

A-5

22 — Steep Turns

1. 45°

2. Left turn

3. Decrease the angle of bank first, then increase back pressure on the yoke to raise the nose. Once you regain your desired altitude, roll back to the desired angle of bank.

4. 20°

5. True

GROUND REFERENCE MANEUVERS

23 — Rectangular Course

1. Standard traffic pattern

2. True

3. 45°

4. Abeam the crosswind segment of the field boundary

5. The turn from the upwind leg to the crosswind leg

24 — S-Turns

1. The ground reference line should be oriented perpendicular, or 90°, to the wind direction.

2. False

3. It will decrease.

4. When flying from a tailwind to a headwind the groundspeed decreases. Therefore, the angle of bank should also be decreased as the turn progresses. In this way, the ground track will be a uniform semicircle.

5. True

25 — Turns Around A Point

1. To the left

2. 45°

3. When headed directly downwind

4. When headed directly upwind

5. ± 100 feet

ANSWERS

PERFORMANCE TAKEOFFS AND LANDINGS

26 — SHORT-FIELD TAKEOFF AND CLIMB

1. The usable runway length is short and/or the runway available for takeoff is restricted by obstructions at the departure end.

2. 50 feet

3. False

4. This procedure enables you to determine that the engine is functioning properly before you take off from a field where power availability is critical and distance to abort a takeoff is limited.

5. A premature nose-high attitude produces more drag and results in a longer takeoff roll. In addition, if the airplane lifts off too soon, it may stall, settle back to the runway or hit the obstacle.

27 — SHORT-FIELD APPROACH AND LANDINGS

1. When there is a relatively short landing area or when an approach must be made over obstacles which limit the available landing area.

2. Steeper

3. Full flaps allow a steeper descent angle without increasing airspeed.

4. True

5. The airplane may touch down too far beyond the runway threshold or the roll-out may exceed the available landing area.

28 — SOFT-FIELD TAKEOFF AND CLIMB

1. To transfer the weight of the airplane from the landing gear to the wings as quickly and smoothly as possible to eliminate drag caused by surfaces such as tall grass, soft dirt, or snow.

2. Any surface that measurably retards acceleration during the takeoff roll.

3. True

4. The airplane may assume an extremely nose-high attitude, which can cause the tail skid to come in contact with the runway.

5. Allow the airplane to accelerate in level flight, within ground effect, to V_X.

Answers

29 — Soft-Field Approach and Landing

1. To ease the weight of the airplane from the wings to the main landing gear as gently and slowly as possible, keeping the nosewheel off the soft surface during most of the landing roll.

2. To allow the airplane to touch down at a minimum speed

3. To dissipate forward speed

4. False

5. C

SPECIAL FLIGHT OPERATIONS

30 — Attitude Instrument Flying

1. The attitude indicator

2. False

3. False

4. Apply right rudder as necessary to control the left-turning tendency.

5. By adjusting pitch attitude

6. 2,050 feet

7. 15°

8. The turn coordinator

9. Simultaneously, add power and lower the nose

10. To avoid increased load factor

31 — Night Operations

1. True

2. Turn on the anticollision light, position lights, or other aircraft lights.

3. Because the narrow beam of the taxi light does not illuminate the areas to the left and right of the airplane.

4. Use the flight instruments in conjunction with outside visual reference to maintain a normal climb attitude.

5. Calmly, but immediately, reference the flight instruments to initiate a 180°, standard rate turn to fly out of the weather.